Politics of Indebtedness of Indigenous People

Politics of Indebtedness of Indigenous People

Study of Purulia District

Binoda Kumar Mishra

Maulana Abul Kalam Azad Institute of Asian Studies, Kolkata

SHIPRA

₹ 550; US $27.50

ISBN: 978-81-7541-641-3

First Published in India in 2012

Politics of Indebtedness of Indigenous People: Study of Purulia District

Published by:
SHIPRA PUBLICATIONS
H.O.: LG 18-19, Pankaj Central Market, Patparganj,
I.P. Ext., Delhi-110092, Tel: 91-11-2223 5152, 2223 6152
Br.Off.: 4617/18, Ansari Road, Darya Ganj,
New Delhi-110002, Tel: 6594 6453, 9810522367
E-mail: info@shiprapublications.com
www.shiprapublications.com

Acknowledgements

I am indebted to Maulana Abul Kalam Azad Institute of Asian Studies (MAKAIAS), Kolkata for allowing me to work on the subject. The book is the culmination of my efforts for a period of three years. During this period I sought the help of some institutions and a good number of people.

I am indebted to Prof. Jayanta Kumar Ray, the Chairman of the MAKAIAS Executive Council for showing faith in me and encouraging me throughout my association with the Institute. I am indebted in the same manner to Prof. H.S. Vasudevan for his encouragement and critical academic inputs he provided from time to time.

Working with colleagues at the institute was a pleasure. Their help was forthcoming at any point I needed. The staff of MAKAIAS library, administrative staff, headed by Dr. P.K. Sengupta saw to it that no researcher faces any trouble in carrying out his/her research. They extended all kinds of support I needed. I am thankful to all of them.

I used the libraries of Jawaharlal Nehru University, Teen Murthy in Delhi and National Library at Kolkata. The staff at all these places extended all their support in a professional manner. During the field work a host of people eagerly extended their support. It is not possible to mention all of them here but I would fail in my duty if I do not express my gratitude to Ms. Mahasweta Devi, Shri Gopi Balhav Sing Deo, Shri Prashanta Rakshit and Deepak Barpanda for going out of their ways to help me in collecting information from the study universe. I am grateful to all of them. My thanks are due to the field researchers who collected quantifiable data from the field in a vicious environment enduring hardship of the climate ad risking their lives in the volatile security environment.

Lastly, I am thankful to my daughter Sneha and to my wife Ishani who took upon themselves the responsibilities of the house allowing me to devote time to my research.

Lastly, despite the effort of all these people, there would be shortcomings in many aspects which are entirely mine.

Dr. Binoda Kumar Mishra

Contents

Introduction

The term politics is often used in a pejorative sense in India in reference to development and using the term "politics of indebtedness" will create the natural confusion that this study may be delving into the role of political class in creating the condition of indebtedness for certain section of the population. On the contrary, the study uses the term politics in its functional definition as "process of authoritative allocation of values"[1] Thus the study attempts to look into the entire process through which values are distributed in the society and argues that it is this process that has forced the indigenous people into the condition indebtedness. Taking the tribals of Purulia district of West Bengal as a case study, it shows that while rest of the society gained from the general process of national development, the indigenous population of this district have become the victims of this process of development and have been lured into the condition of indebtedness from their original condition of self sufficiency.

It is noted that the incidence of poverty fluctuated but showed no sustained decline in the first two and a half decades of independence. Since late 1970s however, the proportion of poor has been declining. Available statistics shows that the proportion of people living below poverty line has decreased from 51.3 per cent in the year 1977-78 to 26.1 per cent in the year 1999-2000 in the country.[2] Contrary to the measures of assessing the poverty at a national level, the region of Purulia is witnessing the trends of increasing poverty. In terms of work participation, there is a negative growth in this district if a comparison is made between the last two censuses. In 1991 the percentage of main workers in proportion to the total population was 35.35 per cent, which reduced to 25.45 in the census year 2001. Correspondingly, there has been an increase in the marginal workers in proportion to the total population of the district. The number of marginal workers has increased from 7.80 per cent to 19 per cent within the last two census years. Purulia thus ranks 11th in the state in terms of Human Development Index.[3] A region with a poor Human Development Index (HDI) will tend to have a greater divide between various segments of the society. Providing indigenous people, an access to basic needs such as food, shelter and clothing have always been foreseen by the support agencies. But the effectiveness of such interventions depends on certain factors such as: recognition of the rights of the indigenous people over the local resources; proper identification of needs, and strong political will at the local as well as state level.

This western district of West Bengal has earned fame for its poverty and of late for militant upsurge. Poverty is conspicuous in the district and so is exploitation of the poor. One has to reflect on the fact that why has there not been a dent to the poverty situation in the district in spite of interventions by the state as well as the central government for nearly six decades? More so of the fact, that in addition, there has also been huge support and funding from generous international aid agencies.

Several studies have shown that poverty was never new to the indigenous people of this district. Most of the SC and ST population being landless, earned their livelihood by working as agricultural labourers. The topography and geography of the district not being suitable for intensive agriculture, provided only three months of employment to the agricultural labourers. Rest of the year, there being no other job opportunity, these labourers were living on borrowings from the landlords or in some cases from moneylenders other than the landlords. This pattern of borrowings caused indebtedness that moved in a yearly circle. This established fact of the lives of the indigenous people of Purulia was expected to change by the extensive coal mining under the 'care' of the government. The coal mines required large number of labour force which was expected to work symbiotically for the government and for the landless poor of the district. Ironically, things have gone worse for these people. A new class of thoroughly professional and extremely organised '*aliens*' (*read also social parasites, brokers, etc.*), have emerged to feast on the earnings of the poor.

Though the natives got a better job opportunity in the form of working in the mines, there has been no change in their condition of poverty, rather their indebtedness has increased. Along with the legal mines there are numerous illegal mines and the labour force engaged in the illegal mines far outnumbers the labour force of the legal (Government) mines. There is some social and economic security for the labourers working in the government controlled mines but there is no such security for those working in the illegal mines. Native poor are made to work in these high risk mines with a meagre remuneration which ultimately is taken away from them in various 'mysterious' ways. The mines attracted 'aliens' to the district who, taking advantage of the ignorance of the natives, have taken upon the role of moneylenders. To add further to the plight of these indigenous people, the forest policies and the rise of the forest based business class have largely alienated the indigenous people from the forest, leaving them without their primary occupation of sustainable collection of non-timber forest produce and earning a livelihood out of it.

The political system seems to be indifferent to the condition of these populations and it is even seen that the local politicians in some cases have joined hands with the inward migrants and sacrificed the interests of the natives in favour of the new moneyed middle-class for political purposes. It seems that the entire socio-economic and political system is manipulated to facilitate the exploitation of the indigenous people. Tribals are being estranged from the forest, marginal farmers are being alienated from their lands and the workers are being deprived of their rightful earnings. In simplistic terms, the growing impoverishment of the indigenous people of this district can broadly be attributed to: (a) cross cultural barriers; (b) socio-economic disadvantage; (c) indifferences of the political leaders and the bureaucracy; and (d) legacies of the past.

Existing Research

The poverty situation in India and in West Bengal has been highlighted in many researches undertaken from time to time. It has been generally accepted that poverty is more pronounced among the lower lungs of the society such as the SC and ST communities. The high incidence of poverty among these sections is attributed to their occupational structure, educational status and expenditure patterns (Kunal Sen & Ira N. Gang & Myeong-Su Yu, 2002).

Poverty in Indian villages is often perceptive. Feeling of increasing poverty, despite in increase in the income of the villagers has been in reference to the income of the richer classes in the villages of West Bengal (Beck, 1994). The much flaunted land reforms did not have equal effect in all the districts of West Bengal. Land ceiling laws had no direct impact on all the villages of West Bengal, because in certain villages no land was declared as surplus and vested with the Government for redistribution. There was, however, one important indirect effect. It led to the large-scale eviction of tenants by landowners (Chattopadhyay, 1992). Other weaknesses which came to the forefront are: (a) neglect of wage demands of the other major poor stratum namely, agricultural labourers; (b) alienation of land from the sharecroppers or redistributed landholders; (c) paying little attention to gender inequality in succession acts of land ownership or redistribution of land titles; (d) erosion of democracy at grassroots levels; and (e) neglect of action in case of complementary inputs. Also, it shows the opportunity cost of not taking appropriate actions along with land reforms, the most important of which is the lack of diversification of crop and other rural industries. (Shanghai Poverty Conference: Case Study Summary India: Lessons from the Land Reform Movement in West Bengal, 2003)

The lower sections of the society have a low income status despite having high work participation per family. Research shows that the families belonging to SC and ST communities in West Bengal have high work participation but low income due to the nature of job these people are engaged in (Planning Commission, 2005). Tribal people are being systematically excluded, across a range of resources and agro-ecological zones, from resources to which they have probably customarily had access for generations (Tony Beck, 1994). The breaking of long term patron client-relationship that existed in traditional Indian societies, has led to loss of a stable income for the lower class service providing sections of the society (Wiser and Wiser, 1971, Wadley and Derr 1989). It has also been argued that the traditional farm labour arrangement in Indian villages was advantageous to the agricultural labourers (Breman, 1993). In the district of Purulia this system often led to bonded labour and caused forced migration and at times selling of girls to the landlords (Chaudhury, 1976). The policies of the Left front Government of West Bengal are no longer radical and do not care for the lower sections of the society. In favour of the numerical strength of the middle class of the rural areas the Left Front Government has sacrificed the interests of the landless for political reasons (D. Bhattacharyya, 1999). Government inaction to the conditions of the indigenous people is well documented. In numerous works Mahasveta Devi and her organisation (Paschim Banga Kheria Sabar Kalyan Samiti) have recorded the atrocities against the ST population and the government remains a mute spectator.

Rationale of the Study

The above mentioned studies are no doubt useful for their portrayal of the condition of impoverishment of the indigenous population. But all these studies are more descriptive in nature and try to explain the situation in simplistic terms. There is hardly any attempt to relate one factor with the other in order to explain the poverty continuum in the district for the indigenous people in comparison to the newly formed class largely comprising of mostly alien inward migrants. Further, no research has focused on the potential conflict between the natives and the inward migrants. The impact of mining on the lives of the natives has also largely been ignored. Politicisation of educational institutions and their impact on the lives of the indigenous people have never attracted any attention. The problem of militant uprising in this district has not been seen as a probable outcome of the present exploitative socio-economic structure. Therefore, a comprehensive analysis of all the variables that can have role in perpetual indebtedness of the natives makes a potential area of research.

Study Objectives

In order to provide these '*marginalized yet mainstream communities*' with the opportunities and access to better livelihood, a holistic approach in identifying and assessing the socio-political issues related to development is most essential for policy planning and implementation. The proposed study envisages identifying, assessing and analysing the issues related to poverty, deprivation, alienation and increasing pauperisation of the indigenous communities of Purulia district. It shall be carried out on the basic premise of the socio-economic, and geo-politico status of indigenous people. Some of the key developmental issues that were foreseen to be studied are: deficit-induced indebtedness leading to loss of control over private resources; insecure or lack of land tenure among some of the poorest groups; dysfunctional manipulated educational system and muted political mobilisation; declining availability and control over common property and forest resources; and below subsistence production.

The specific objectives of the proposed research were as follows:

1. To study the socio-economic status of the native/indigenous (tribal) population of Purulia.
2. To find out the reasons for *poverty continuum* for the tribals.
3. To evaluate the extent of effect of new social milieu on the life styles of the natives.
4. To verify the effectiveness of the interventions in the context of dealing with alienation, conflict resolution, poverty alleviation and empowerment of the indigenous communities.
5. To examine the potential of the socio–cultural, geo-political and economic conflicts between the indigenous people and the inward migrants in the district.
6. To devise policy alternatives for alleviating the socio-economic profile of the indigenous people of this district.

Research Questions

The research questions that have emerged on the basis of the review of the existing literature and the objectives of the study are:

1. What are the historical reasons for present pauperisation of the tribals?
2. Whether inward migration has led to negative sanskritisation of the indigenous communities?
3. What are the means of exploitation of the tribals?
4. Is there a causal relation between the poverty continuum and the militant uprising in the district?
5. Is the present militant uprising a desperate reaction of the indigenous communities?
6. Have the intervention systems, been, able to identify any alternative methods, which could be used while dealing with exploitation of indigenous communities?

Methodology

The proposed study would primarily be exploratory in nature. Empirical research method is proposed to be used in data collection. Both secondary and primary information will be used in the study.

Secondary information will be collected for building the historical context of the problem and preparing the analytical framework. Existing literature, published government documents at the state and district level will be searched for such information.

Since the study involved many questions that need first hand information, primary data would be collected from the study universe. Primary information shall be collected by formulating missions to the area for studying the communities through standard methods of social sciences including participatory appraisal and case study. This will be complemented by additional information gathered by periodical reformulation studies from village men and women, different government offices and non-governmental organizations (NGOs) through direct, indirect, empirical and statistical data collection techniques. Quantifiable data shall be collected by using research techniques such as interviews with the help of semi-structured research schedules.

Sampling Design

Social science surveys involving large number of people and vast geographical area have to be carried out on the basis of sampling procedure. Though total coverage is a welcome effort, time factor and resources may make it difficult to go in for study of the entire population distributed over a wide area. Therefore, sustained and well designed need based sampling techniques based on standard principles of statistical analysis shall be undertaken during the investigation in the region.

For collection of primary data, three blocks were chosen on the ground of presence of tribal population in comparison to other districts. The blocks chosen were Bandwan, Manbazar-I and Manbazar-II. In terms of presence of tribals in absolute numbers Bandwan, Manbazar-II and Manbazar-I occupy first, second and fourth place respectively. Minimum four villages from each block were chosen randomly for survey. But keeping the focus of study in mind it was attempted to cover as many types of tribal community as possible from the three blocks. Thus, the initial plan of collecting same number of data from each village was compromised. There was a practical constraint also that in some cases limited the number of respondents from each village below the targeted number. The tribal villages being scattered and comprising of small number of households the target number of respondents were not found in some villages during the study period. Therefore, the study has ended up covering 16 villages from three blocks.

Constraints of Research

At the time of conceptualisation of the research the law and order situation of the district was not as bad as it was during the time of actual collection of primary data. Given the fact that there has been an escalation of violence by and related to 'Maoists' and the problems there from, conducting field investigation proved to be not only difficult but also dangerous to life. However, after lot of persuasion and effort, the locals agreed to talk to the field researchers. But considering the level of fear the local community is suffering from the information shared by the respondents cannot be vouched to be entirely unbiased or uninfluenced. The second constraint of research encountered during collection of primary data was the level of awareness of the respondent group. The research schedule prepared to collect quantifiable data was though helpful but proved to be insufficient to extract the desired quality of data. The gap has thus been attempted to be bridged from the impressions gathered through intensive and extensive interactions with the respondents. The third and most important problem that was faced during the field survey was absence of respondents from the village. The large scale migration of the tribals to other parts of the state and outside had resulted in a deserted look of the villages. Apart from these unintended problems of research, one of the weaknesses of the research remains to be non-coverage of the local politicians of the ruling party. It was noticed that most of the political leaders of the ruling party were absent during the period of the survey not in fear of any questions from any research team or journalist but due to the fear of being the text target of the very targeted so called Maoist forces. So the opinion of the political class largely remains unrepresented in the study.

Profile of the Respondents

- No.of Blocks 3
- No.of villages 16
- No.of Respondents 120
- Literacy level of the respondents standard V
- Average annual Income 5,000 to 10,000 Rupees
- Average size of the family 4.20
- Average literacy level of the children < V
- Average size of the landholding 1 acre
- Average monthly expenditure 1,000 to 1,500 Rupees

Notes and References

1. David Easton (1953), *The Political System: An Inquiry into the State of Political Science*, (New York: Alfred A. Knopf, p. 129)
2. *Economic Survey 2004-2005*, Government of India.
3. West Bengal Human Development Report, http://www.undp.org.in/hdrc/events/Constn_Gndr_SHDRs/JayathiGosh.ppt.

I
Communities of Purulia
Identifying the Indigenous People

I. Definition of Indigenous People in National and Regional Context

An indigene is literally someone or something that is native to or originating from a given place. Therefore, when indigenous is used purely as an adjective, an indigenous people is a group regarded as "coming from" a given place. In this broad sense almost any person or group is indigenous to some location or other. However, the term 'indigenous people' has a much narrower meaning. The term 'indigenous people' has no universal, or fixed definition. Several formulations have been put forward by important internationally recognised organizations, such as the United Nations, the International Labour Organization and the World Bank.[1] Drawing on these formulations, a working definition of "indigenous *peoples*[2]" has been developed. This definition provides for certain criteria which would seek to include cultural groups who have an historical continuity or association with a given region, or parts of a region, and who formerly or currently inhabit a particular region either:

- Before its subsequent colonisation or annexation; or
- Alongside other cultural groups during the formation of a nation-state; or
- Independently or largely isolated from the influence of the claimed governance by a nation-state,

and who furthermore

- Have maintained at least in part their distinct linguistic,

> cultural and social/organizational characteristics, and in doing so remain differentiated in some degree from the surrounding populations and dominant culture of the nation-state.[3]

To the above, a criterion is usually added to also include:

- Peoples who are self-identified as indigenous, and those recognised as such by other groups.[4]

Other related terms for indigenous peoples include aborigines, native peoples, first peoples, Fourth World, first nations and autochthonous (this last term is a derivation from Greek, meaning "sprung from the earth").

Examining the nature and status of their interactions with other communities can further refine the identification of people as indigenous under these terms. These other, external communities or nation-states are those having some degree of association, claim or control over the same territory inhabited (or formerly inhabited) by the indigenous group. In this relationship the status of the indigenous people can in most instances be characterised as being effectively marginalized, isolated and/or as forming a minority, when compared to other groups from whom they are distinct, or the nation-state as a whole. They have limited participation and influence over external policies concerning their territorial, environmental and societal governance. This situation persists even in cases where the indigenous population outnumbers the other inhabitants of the region or state.

Characteristics common across many indigenous groups are; present or historical reliance upon subsistence-based production (based on pastoral, agricultural and/or hunting and gathering techniques), and a predominantly non-urbanised society. Indigenous societies may be either settled in a given location or exhibit a nomadic lifestyle across a large territory. Indigenous societies are found in every inhabited climate zone and continent.

Indigenous Populations in India

Identifying Tribals

The constitution of India identifies the indigenous peoples as 'tribes'. But the criteria for identifying tribes have not been fixed as is evident from the fluctuations in the numbers of the tribal population in the country. India's 1931 census enumerated 22 million tribal people, in 1941 only 10 million were counted, but by 1961 some 30 million and in 1991 nearly 68 million tribal members were included. The differences among the figures reflect changing census criteria.[5] This is because "the scientific or theoretical considerations were never allowed to displace the administrative or political ones".[6] "Tribes as a social formation may be identified in two ways: firstly, as a stage in the history of evolution of human civilisation; secondly, as a society organised on the basis of kinship ties which enables them to be a multifunctional grouping".[7] In India, tribals are defined in reference to the cultural practices of certain groups in relation to the mainstream Hindu cultural practices.

According to the 2001 census, scheduled tribes constitute 8.2 per cent of Indian national population.[8] Most tribes are concentrated in forest areas and have limited political or economic significance to the nation. Historically, the primary source of the economy of most tribes has been subsistence agriculture or hunting and gathering. They prefer isolationism and thus maintain minimal contact with outsiders. Their interaction with the outsiders is limited to trade for the few necessities they lacked, such as salt and iron. In the early 20th century, however, large areas fell into the hands of non-tribals, on account of improved transportation and communications.

Around 1900, many regions were opened by the government to settlement through a scheme by which inward migrants received ownership of land free in return for cultivating it.[9] For tribal people, however, land was often viewed as a common resource, free to whoever needed it. By the time tribals realised the necessity of obtaining formal land titles, they had lost the opportunity to lay claim to lands that might rightfully have been considered theirs. The colonial and post-independence regimes belatedly realised the necessity of protecting tribals from the predatory practice of the outsiders and prohibited the sale of tribal lands to non-tribals. But there remain some loopholes that are taken advantage of by the relatively advanced non-tribal population and alienation of tribal land still persists in one form or the other.

In the 1970s, tribal people again came under intense land pressure, especially in central India. Migration into tribal lands increased dramatically, as tribal people lost title to their lands in many ways – lease, forfeiture from debts, or bribery of land registry officials.[10] Other non-tribals simply squatted, or even lobbied governments to classify them as tribal to allow them to compete with the formerly established tribes. In any case, many tribal members became landless labourers in the 1960s and 1970s, and regions that a few years earlier had been the exclusive domain of tribes started having an increasingly mixed population of tribals and non-tribals.

Improved communications, roads with motorized traffic, and more frequent government intervention resulted in the increased contact of the tribals with outsiders. Commercial highways and cash crops frequently drew non-tribal people into remote areas. By the 1960s and 1970s, the resident non-tribal shopkeeper was a permanent feature of many tribal villages. Since shopkeepers often sell goods on credit (demanding high interest), many tribal members have been drawn deeply into debt or mortgaged their land. Merchants also encourage tribals to grow cash crops (such as cotton or castor-oil plants), which increases tribal dependence on the market for basic necessities. Indebtedness is so extensive that although such transactions are illegal, traders sometimes 'sell' their debtors to other merchants, much like indentured peons.[11]

Tribes in the Himalayan foothills have not been as hard-pressed by the intrusions of non-tribals as in the rest of the country. Historically, their political status was always distinct from the rest of India. Until the British colonial period, there was little effective control by any of the empires centred in peninsular India over the autonomous feuding tribes populated the Himalayan region. The British, in efforts to protect the sensitive northeast frontier, followed a policy dubbed the "Inner Line"; non-tribal people were allowed into the areas only with special permission. Post-independence governments have continued the policy, protecting the Himalayan tribes as part of the strategy to secure their identity and culture or may be simply to secure the border with China.

Government policies on forest reserves have affected the tribals profoundly. Government efforts to reserve forests have precipitated armed resistance on the part of the tribal peoples involved. Intensive exploitation of forests has often meant allowing outsiders to cut large areas of trees (while the original tribal inhabitants were restricted from cutting), and ultimately replacing mixed forests capable of sustaining tribal life with single-product plantations.[12]

Indigenous Populations of Purulia

The tribal belt of Eastern India comprising Orissa, Bihar and West Bengal has major concentration of tribal population. "Even though in course of history these tracts have been subject to waves of non-tribal immigrations, intruders, and adventurers, the tribal people inhabiting these areas have always considered themselves indigenous, insider, we group, sons of the soil, aborigines, autochthonous and take great pride in calling themselves as the inheritors of their *abua desum* (their country).[13] They termed the neosettlers, intruders vaguely as *Dikus*. In west Bengal there are 40 scheduled tribes communities[14] of which 9 are major and account for 90 per cent of the total tribal population of the state. They are Santhal, Oraon, Munda, Bhumij, Kora, Mahali, Lodha/Kharia, Bhutia and Malpaharia. Of these major tribal groups, baring Bhutia all other tribal communities are found in the district of Purulia. The group composition of the district is given below in detail.

Santhal

Among the tribes of the district, Santhals are in majority. They are believed to be Dravidians, 'Dramil'.[15] Prior to agriculture based settled life, they were nomads. There is hardly any record to ascertain their origin. But from the popular culture and folksongs whatever can be presented it can be said that the Santhals belonged to a branch of Kharowar community and when they reached the Bankura, Purulia and Mednipur region around late 18th century, they were engaged in battle with the local tribes namely the Bhumij and the Mundas, and finally managed to find a place for settlement in 'Saunte' and thus got the name Santhal. A section of them got sanskritised (in parts of Bihar) and got close to 'Cher' but those who maintained their tribal identity continued to be known as Santhals.

Kurmis

Kurmis are found in UP, Bihar, Chotanagpur, West Bengal and Orissa. They are mostly agriculturists. The origin of this community is debated. According to one account, they are the oldest heirs of the Aryan colonisers. Their physical features in UP and Bihar shows Aryan influence. According to Dalton, Kurmis stayed in the Chotanagpur region from very old times. There are proofs that they fought with

Kol speaking communities, the Bhumijs and the Mundas. Speculations are that by the 19th century, they had completed 52 generations in the region.[16]

The other assumption is provided by Risley. He finds close similarity between the Kurmis of Manbhum and northern Orissa with that of the Bhumij and the Santhal Community. He puts forward three speculations:

i. There are two divisions of Kurmis; one belongs to the Aryan Family and the other the Dravidian community.
ii. The whole community is derived from Aryan community and through physical interaction and demands of occupation changes have come about.
iii. The community is Dravidian and through interaction with the Aryans a section of them developed while those residing in remote areas remained primitive and undeveloped.[17]

Risely semi-spontaneously supports the third proposition. At present there are two divisions of Kurmis namely; the 'Jharia Kurmi' and the 'Maratta Kurmi'. The Jharia Kurmis came to the region much before the Maratta Kurmis who came after the Bargi invasion. Among these Kurmis the Maratta Kurmis are affluent and through sanskritisation have come close to the Hindus and claim to be Kshetriya and Brahmanas but a section of the Kurmis still retain their tribal identity and live in remote jungle areas of the district and are known by various titles.

Bhumij

Dalton argues that before the Aryan invasion some ancient tribes using Kol and Munda languages lived along the riverine tracts of the Ganga. They concentrated in Gorakhpur, Bihar and Sahabad areas. Heirs of this primitive community are divided into various communities – Munda, Khariya, Santhal, Bhumij, Ho, etc. Bhumijata or Bhumij lived along the Kanshai and Subarnrekha rivers. They called themselves as 'sardars'. Earlier they lived in the north of Kanshai but because of interaction with the Aryans (probably Kurmis) they moved down south. There is a close connection of the Bhumij with the Mundas. Risely thinks Bhumij were actually pure Mundas. However, the Ayhodhya hills became a geographical barrier between the two communities.

The Mundas lived to the east of the Ayodhya and never interacted with the Bhumij. In course of time, the Mundas adopted Hindu customs and mastered Bengali language and detached themselves from the main community. The Bhumij on the other hand, maintained their own distinct characteristics and developed into another community. There are no Bhumij narrations on long journeys to other destinations or accounts of settling in other areas. Therefore they can be taken as very old inhabitants of this region. Risely also thinks that the majority of the Ghatowal community in Manbhum and Dhalbhum were once the Bhumij. He adds that the royals of Dhalbhum were also Bhumij.

Bhumij, being an ancient community, are actually divided into various divisions and subdivisions. There are six such divisions – *Desi, Tamariya Mura or Manik Mura, Shikhariya or Meno, Patkumia, shelo and Borabhumiya.* Amongst these divisions some of them are indicative of their original settlements viz., *Tamar* (*Tamariya Mura*), *Shikharbhum* (*Shikhariya*), *Patkum* (*Patkumia*) and *Borabhum* (*Borabhumiya*). Risley speaks of twenty subdivisions – *Budda, Kurkutia, Baroda, Bhuiya* (Fish), *Chandil, Gulgu* (Fish), *Handsa* (Swan), *Hembrom,* Jaroo (Bird), *Kashyap* (Tortoise), *Lengo* (Mushroom), *Nag* (Snake), *Abarshari* (Bird), *Pila, Sagma, Shalrishi, Shandilya* (Bird), *Shaola, Tesha* (Bird), *Tumrat* (Bottle Gourd), *Tuti* (Vegetable). There are nine other sub divisions discovered later – *Uburshandilya, Jugi, Sama, Parasa, Saithiyan, Deo, Sirka, Koira and Kaori.* All these subdivisions are known as 'Gotras' Actually, there seem to be 55 such 'Gotras' Bhumij settlements were spread in nine directions, they are, Panchasardari, Satrokhani, Tinsua, Dhadka, Bangurda, Sarberia, dubroji, Ghartali and Kumaripur. Therefore it shows that 'Gotras' are not confined to geographical limitations. Moreover, as shown above, 'Gotras' are closely related to 'totems'; every member of the 'Gotra' carries the relevant totem – object, animal or plant and is restricted from killing or wasting the same. At present times, 'Gotras' are not maintained strictly, they are found at *asthi* graveyard stones. Bhumij have four titles – *Manki, Matkun, Mura, and Sardar or Singh Sardar.*

War had been the primary occupation of the Bhumij. In the eighteenth and nineteenth century, in the clashes that took place between the indigenous communities and the British, the primary role had been played by the Bhumij. They were also infamous for attacking and looting. Large parts of southern Manbhum were taken over by the

Bhumij, the areas include – Ghatowal, Sardar, Tabedar, Sorial and Dighoar. Risley also thinks that the Zamindars of Borabhumm, Dhalbhumm, Manbhum, Patbhum and Bagmundi were once Bhumij, all goes to say that they may have extended their power to these regions also.

The Bhumij are often called a disintegrating community. Once they were known as the aristocratic community having money to promote cultural activities like the *Chou Naach*, of Purulia. They have been losing economically and taken over by poverty. To maintain their status they have sold all their habited and uninhabited lands to Kurmi Mahatos, Oriya Brahmins and other communities. Therefore, agriculture has ceased to be their primary occupation. At present, mixed village population has affected their unity and ways of community characteristics. Moreover, Bhumij societies have also changed over time and well off bhumij have adopted Hindu ways of life and would like to call themselves 'Rajputs'. Probably the only remnant of their glorious tradition is the process in which they bury the 'asthis' of their near and dear ones. This process bears a resemblance to the Munda process of burial. At present the centre of Bhumij tradition and identity is at Borabajar and the king is said to belong to the same community.

Bauris

Bauris are the largest amongst tribes included in the Scheduled list. Anthropologists are not sure of their origin. It seems once, the Bauris lived in the Shergarh Parganas in Burdwan district of West Bengal. Following the discovery of mines, the workers began to move in and the Bauris were forced to move out. They settled to the Southern banks of Damodar and as a result they are concentrated in Bankura and Purulia. Amongst the nine divisions of the Bauris, two of them are really old – Panchakoti and Shikharya or Gobariya; they are indicative of the close association of Bauris with Purulia. Bauris have picked up traits of both Hindus and Muslims, it depends on their neighbourhood. The larger section has adopted Hindu social traits. However, at least one of their subdivisions and a title speaks of Muslim references. The four subdivisions are *Alimon or Aliman, Kashyap, Madhukulya and* Majhi. Titles include, *Digha, Mandal, Majhi, Maulavi, Bauri and* Paramanik. *Aliman* and *Maulavi* are indicative of Muslim influences on them. Bauris are very underdeveloped and the level of literacy is extremely poor. Their occupation pattern is evenly distributed between cultivation and labour and men and women work equally.

Sarak or Sharak or Shrabok

Sharaks resided in Manbhum and were known to be the creators of ancient Jain artefacts; they are also associated with ancient Jain archaeological sites in Purulia. They also started copper mining in the region. Manbhum is now divided into Purulia and Dhanbad – they are settled in both the districts. Sharaks are also found in Burdwan, Birbhum, Dumka, Ranchi and Bankura. There is no unanimous opinion of their origin and trajectory of movements.

Sharaks of Manbhum and Ranchi claim that they were the ancient residents of the settlements on the banks of the Saraju River near Gajipur. They were a money lending community but they were also involved in other business activities. The Agarwals seemed to belong to this community, they worshipped Pareshnath. There is no clear explanation as to why they left the place and moved to settle in Manbhum very close to Dhalbhum. One of the kings of Manbhum attracted by the beauty of a Sharak lady moved to Panchet. Some Sharaks of Ranchi are of an entirely different view of their origins, they think that their ancient land is Ogra near Puri. Later, they settled at Chotanagpur region. Sharaks of Burdwan and Birbhum claim to be masons who were invited from Ogra to construct temples. Their craftsmanship is found in the temples of Barakar. Their divisions bear testimony of their ancient identity. The divisions, sub-divisions and gotras have changed over time.

In Purulia, Sharaks are divided into two divisions – 'Choto Shikha' and 'Athero Shikha'. The latter occupy the higher social position, however, marriage between both the sections is allowed. There are seven gotras – *Adi or Adya Deb, Dharma Deb, Rishideb, Shandilya, Kashyap, Anant and Bhradra*. In Birbhum two more gotras are found – *Goutam and* Vyas; in Ranchi, *Batsya* was added. Names of the Gotra speak clearly of the effects of Hindu customs. Apart from Gotras there are *Thaks* or ranks. These are determined according to the occupation. E.A. Gait mentions five such ranks:

1. *Panchakoti* i.e. those living under Panchakot Zamindari;
2. *Nadipario* i.e. all those who crossed into the Damodar and settled in the Western banks of the Damodar;

3. *Birbhumi* or those residing in Birbhum'
4. *Tamario* or those living in the Tamor Parganas under Ranchi districts;and
5. *Tanti Sharak*, living in the Bishnupur Mahakumar in Bankura district.

In Orissa, Sharaks are known as *Sharak Tantis* (Weaver). In the beginning of the twentieth century Sharaks there, have been documented in the census as Buddhists. It is heard that their fathers went from Burdwan to Puri to offer their respects to Jagannath. Puri's king was a Buddhist. He took interest in the Sharaks and gave them land close to the palace to settle. There the Sharaks bear four Gotras – *Adi Deb, Krishna Deb, Hem Deb and Dharma Deb*. The titles they bear have a resemblance with Bengali titles, for example, Chanda, Dutta, Kar and Nandi. Notwithstanding the authenticity of this story, it seems that Sharak settlements in Orissa can be dated to somewhere between 200 B.C. and 400 A.D. Sharak settlements of Manbhum date much earlier.

In West Bengal, Sharaks generally bear the titles of *Majhi, Sharak, Mandal, Singh, Khan, Patra, Layak, Baishnab, Bakshi*, etc. In Sikharbhum, when the Jain kingdom broke down, Sharaks spread to different directions, breaking away from their main community. In the meanwhile, Brahmin culture and Shiva cult were being rejuvenated and Sharaks were absorbed into it. In Orissa, they were following the Dashami Shaiva Community and in West Bengal, Shaiva Dharma was also very important amongst Sharaks. Important meetings in their community take place in Shiva temples of the locality. In Purulia the most famous gathering took place at Dapuniar Shivmandir in Raghuathpur. At the same time, E.A. Gait has referred to marriage customs/characteristics that are indicative of Buddhist influences, but Hindu religion is predominant.

Agriculture is their primary occupation. Sharaks are comparatively educated than other indigenous communities. It is noteworthy to mention in this context that a section of women of the community are also educated.

Brahmins

In Purulia, there are five categories of Brahmins – *Rarhi, Kanyakubja, Maithili, Madhyasreni and Utkal*. They are concentrated in areas under

Raghunathpur and Kashipur police stations. Popular narrations say that Kashipur kings patronised the Brahmins and a Brahmin settlement grew up close to Kashipur. Other Brahmin settlements grew up in a similar fashion in Borabajar, Manbajar and Joipur. Other settlements are of recent times and they are related to occupations.

Rarhi Brahmins are related to the Adishpur and Kanyakubja popular folk tale. Five Brahmins in response to Adishpur's invitation came and settled in the Western banks of the Bhagirath around the 11th century B.C. It is believed that another five Brahmins were given permission to settle there and given landed property. Amongst them, one was Khitish, who decided to settle in Panchakot. Bhattanarayan belongs to one of the latter generations of Khitish's dynasty. Bhattanaryan's sixteen sons established settlements in Ghoshal village along the southern banks of the Barakar River. *Rarhi Brahmins* bear five gotras – *Shandilya, Kashyap, Batsya or Bhargav, Shabarno and Bharadraj*. They have been living in Purulia since ancient times and have made substantial contribution towards the improvement of the general life style in Purulia.

Kanyakubja Brahmins or the *Kanauj Brahmins* are settled in the northern part of Purulia close to Kashipur. Their conventions and customs follow *Shukla Yajur Veda.* Kashipur kings provided them with land and a Brahmin also became their 'guru'. The king's dynasty got baptised in Ram mantra and then became the king's priest. *Kanauj Brahmins* claim that they lived in Ayodhya as the priest of Ram. However, it seems that those came to Purulia were actually from Bihar. One cannot ignore that present Purulia or erstwhile Manbhum was actually a part of Bihar. *Maithili Brahmins* are in majority in the north-western part of Purulia – Jhalda, Para, Joipur and Neturia region. In the district there is no distinction between the *Kanauj and Maithili Brahmins*. It is believed that Brahmins brought by the Kashipur kings to the district and a second section of the Brahmins are believed to have migrated from Orissa in search of livelihoods during famines in Orissa.

Other Communities

Other communities in the district include Mahali, Kora/Mudi, Birhor, Oraon, Sabar (kheria) Rajwar, Hari, Dom, Chamar, Dhoba, Gowala, Lohar or Kamar, the Munda and Kora communities who do not have significant implications for the population profile of the district.

II. Inward migration during colonial period through permanent settlement

The first form of migration to the tribal areas took place through the process of migration on invitation of farmers from the coastal areas. This was facilitated by the provision of permanent settlement policy of the colonial administration. Under the permanent settlement system, introduced around 1793, feudal lords (zamindars jagirdars, etc.) were declared proprietors of the land on condition of fixed revenue payments to the British regime. Peasants were transformed into tenant farmers, and rents were collected by serried ranks of intermediaries below the level of zamindars. This system prevailed over most of North India, including present-day Uttar Pradesh (except Avadh and Agra), Bihar, West Bengal, most of Orissa, and Rajasthan (except Jaipur and Jodhpur), and covered around 57 per cent of the total area cultivated. The grid of more profits from the land made the Zamindars or the owners of land, invite farmers from the coastal areas who were better cultivators and promised to yield more than the indigenous cultivators who were primitive in techniques on cultivation. Slowly and steadily this initial migration led to further migration imposing pressure on the indigenous population of the tribal areas and the resources. The inward migrants, by dint of their advantage of better awareness linked up the local resources and the market outside. It may not have been intentional, but the tribals were kept outside the chain of resource outflow from the locality. The inward migrant farmers turned themselves into traders and traded in local resources.

III. Inward Migration after Independence

Migration after independence was due to the process of development than any other reason. The district boasts of its natural resources attracting exploration by entrepreneurs and the government. Among major resources, coal and iron ore are prominent. These important natural resources were considered essential for the development of the nation and large projects have been undertaken to tap these resources. Along with government others who migrated into the district are traders. This second phase of migration created urban centres in the district and increased the interaction of the tribals with the civilised world. With the inward migration came alien culture and thus the process of sanskritisation of the tribals began.

IV. Composition of the Local Society (Changing proportions)

The composition of the local society seems half hazard as the population proportion of the tribal population seems to have fluctuated over the years. The fluctuation in the population is more due to the technique used to identify tribals than actual fluctuation in their presence. However, currently the tribals constitute 18.27 per cent of the total population. In terms of habitation, the tribals still reside in the hinterlands where as the non-tribals reside in accessible areas. But the increase in the non-tribal population is evident from the decrease of the tribal percentage to the total population. Just as a comparison, the tribal percentage in the year 1991 was 19.23 per cent to the total population of the district. In 10 years the tribal population has decreased by nearly 1 per cent though there has been increase in the tribal population in absolute terms.[18]

Purulia is well known as a drought prone district and falls within the semi-arid region of the state. Cultivation of this district is predominantly mono-cropped. Out of total geographical land 52.47 per cent are used for agriculture. 29.69 per cent are under forest coverage (including social forestry) and 10.15 per cent are identified as Wasteland. Soil erosion is the most prominent phenomenon of the district resulting huge deposition of fertile soil in the valley region. Vast areas of land remained uncultivable wasteland. Out of the total agricultural holding about 73 per cent belongs to small and marginal farmers having scattered and fragmented smallholding. About 90 per cent of the population lives in villages and about 44 per cent of the rural population is below poverty line.

Notes and References

1. In 1972 the United Nations Working Group on Indigenous Populations (WGIP) accepted as a preliminary definition a formulation put forward by Mr. José Martinez Cobo, Special Rapporteur on Discrimination against Indigenous Populations: *Indigenous populations are composed of the existing descendants of the peoples who inhabited the present territory of a country wholly or partially at the time when persons of a different culture or ethnic origin arrived there from other parts of the world, overcame them, by conquest, settlement or other means, reduced them to a non-dominant or colonial condition; who today live more in*

conformity with their particular social, economic and cultural customs and traditions than with the institutions of the country of which they now form part, under a state structure which incorporates mainly national, social and cultural characteristics of other segments of the population which are predominant. This definition has some limitations which were subsequently noted by the organization. The definition applies mainly to pre-colonial populations, and would likely exclude other isolated or marginal societies. In 1983 the WGIP enlarged this definition (FICN. 41Sub.211983121 Adds. para. 3 79) to include the following criteria: *(a) they are the descendants of groups, which were in the territory at the time when other groups of different cultures or ethnic origin arrived there; (b) precisely because of their isolation from other segments of the country's population they have almost preserved intact the customs and traditions of their ancestors which are similar to those characterised as indigenous; (c) they are, even if only formally, placed under a state structure which incorporates national, social and cultural characteristics alien to their own.* In 1986 it was further added that *any individual who identified himself or herself as indigenous and was accepted by the group or the community as one of its members was to be regarded as an indigenous person* (E/CN.4/Sub.2/1986/7/Add.4. para.381). The draft Universal Declaration on the Rights of the Indigenous Peoples prepared by the DWIG does not provide a specific definition of indigenous peoples or populations. According to the Chairperson, Ms. Erica Irene Daes, Rapporteur of the Working Group, this was because "historically, indigenous peoples have suffered, from definitions imposed by others" (E/CN.4/Stib.2/AC.4/1995/3, page 3). A definition as used by the International Labour Organisation (Convention No. 169, concerning the working rights of Indigenous and Tribal Peoples, 1989) applies to: both tribal peoples whose social, cultural and economic conditions distinguish them from other sections of the national community and whose status is regulated wholly or partially by their own customs or traditions or by special laws or regulations, and to peoples who are regarded as indigenous on account of their descent from the populations which inhabit the country at the time of conquest or colonisation. A description of Indigenous Peoples given by the World Bank (operational directive 4.20, 1991) reads as follows: Indigenous Peoples can be identified in particular geographical areas by the presence in varying degrees of the following characteristics: a) close attachment to ancestral territories and to the natural resources in these areas; b) self-identification and identification by others as members of a distinct cultural group; c) an indigenous language, often different from the national language; d) presence of customary social and political institutions; and e) primarily subsistence-oriented production.

2. There is no unanimity on accepting "Community."
3. Indigenous Peoples, *Wikipedia*, http://en.wikipedia.org.
4. *Ibid.*
5. Indian Tribes, http://www.indianchild.com/indian_tribes.htm.
6. Andre Beteille (1991), *Society and Politics in India: Essays in Comparative Perspective*, (London: Athlone Press Ltd., p. 59)
7. B.K. Roy Buman (1989), "Problems and Prospects of Tribal Development in North-East India," *Economic and Political Weekly*, April 1.
8. Census Document, Government of India, 2001, www.censusindia.net.
9. A detailed discussion on the process of land alienation during this period will be undertaken later.
10 Indebtedness has been identified as the main cause of land alienation from the tribals. The process of indebtedness has thus been identified as the main area of focus in this piece of study.
11. Indigenous Peoples, *Op cit.*
12. Guha, Ramachandra (1998), "Detrich Brandis and Indian Forestry," *Village Voices, Forest Choices*, MarkPoffenberger and Betsy McGean, p. 95. For the details of the National Forest Policy, see Ministry of Environment and Forestry (1998), National Forest Policy.
13. S.P. Sihna, "Land Tenure, Ownership and Alienation in Bihar, West Bengal and Orissa," in S.N. Mishra (ed.) (1998), *Antiquity to Modernity in Tribal India Volume 111*, (New Delhi: Inter-India Publications, p. 66)
14. http://www.indiantravelportal.com/west-bengal/
15. E.T. Dalton (1872), *Descriptive Ethnology of Bengal*. Cited in, Arundeb Bhattacharya (1986), *Purulia*, (Calcutta: Pharma Prakasan).
16. Ibid.
17. H.H. Risley (1891), *Tribes and Castes of Bengal*. Cited in Arundeb Bhattacharya (1986), *Purulia*, (Calcutta: Pharma Prakasan).
18. http://purulia.gov.in/district_profile/demography.html. The difference between 1991 and 2001 has been considered because the criteria for identifying tribes in the district were same for the two most recent censuses.

II

Socio-Economic Profile of the Natives

I. State of Life of Scheduled Tribes in India

Adequate level of income and control over physical resources is a necessary prerequisite for ensuring a reasonable quality of life. Of the physical resources, land is the primary resource that contributes to the livelihood status. At the all India level, the average value of the household assets for the STs is more than the SCs though it is far less than the average asset of the other (general) section of the society. In Indian tradition, the tribals were never included in the Hindu structure of the society. The isolationist nature of the tribals never warranted their inclusion into the Hindu fold. But increasing inward migration into the tribal societies and the large-scale migration of the displace migrants into the urban and semi-urban areas called for fixation of status for the tribals and not surprisingly were assigned a position equivalent to the lowest rung of the Hindu social system. According to the Hindu tradition social status is not related to economic achievement.[1] Therefore, the assigned social position of the tribals does not reflect their economic status. As their numerical strength, the economic statue of the tribals have varied over time owing to the differing criteria used in censuses. Economically, the status has also varied though has hardly been able to cross the line of poverty.

According to the NSSO survey of 2006, of the total ST population of rural India 69 per cent are cultivators[2] and according to one study the average size of landholding of tribals is more than twice that of the SC population but there is hardly any difference in favour of the tribals in terms of their economic status. At the national level, 43 per cent of the tribals hold less than one hectare of land in comparison to 63 per cent of SCs in the similar category. One of the explanations for this apparent anomaly is the nature of the land the tribals hold.

Being pushed by the intruding non-tribals time and again for over a period of time, the land, the tribals now own are hilly and least productive in comparison to the plain lands. The second factor affecting the economic condition adversely, despite having landholdings larger than the SC community, is the inequality of distribution.[3] Historically, the inward migrants to the tribal areas were given the prime land for better productivity and revenue for the Zamindars. This caused displacement of the tribals who moved upwards to the hilly and forest areas, which were not suitable for intensive farming.

The data below depicts the profile of the tribals[4]

Table 1

	1991 Census	%	*2001 Census*	%
Total Population	2224577		2536516	
Male Population	1142771	51.37	1298078	51.18
Female Pop.	1081806	48.63	1238438	48.82
Rural Population	2014571	90.56	2281090	89.93
Urban Population	210006	9.44	255426	10.07
Scheduled Caste	430513	19.35	463956	18.29
Scheduled Tribe	427765	19.23	463452	18.27
Sex Ratio	947		954	
Population Density (per sq. km.)	355		405	
Decadal Growth Rate	20.00 (1981-91)		14.02 (1991-2001)	

Source: Purulia district website, http://purulia.gov.in/district_profile/demography.html

Given the fact that apart from 27 per cent of tribals who reported to be landless, all others are engaged in agricultural activity in their own land for some period of the year. Thus the figure cited here is as per the preference of the tribal as to what he considers his primary source of income. Agriculture is naturally preferred as the primary occupation by those who have larger landholdings. It is also the preferred occupation for those who have managed to have their smaller landholdings in such place where intensive farming is possible. In the negative side tribals having relatively larger landholding have also opined that agricultural or non-agricultural wage labour is their primary occupation. There are two explanations for such seemingly irrational choice. First, the quality of the land does not permit viable cultivation in comparison to the requirement of the household. Secondly, tribals who are part of the process of seasonal migration and migrate for increasing their income in comparison to their income from land also prefer to identify agricultural/non-agricultural wage labour as their primary occupation.

Primary Occupation

Occupation	*Percentage*
Agriculture	12
Agricultural Wage Labourer	58
Non-agricultural wage labourer	30

Source: Primary Village Survey.

Changing Occupation of the Tribals

"Since independence, tribal ecological and economical conditions have undergone many changes as result of governmental policies. Rapid industrialization through economic planning, constitutional laws which is responsible for the creation of democratic, secular, and egalitarian society, introduction of land reforms and Community Development Projects (CDP) in tribal areas since 1950's, influences of modern science and technology specially on their pristine practices, all have deeply affected the social, institutional, economic, cultural as well as political structure of tribes of Purulia. Application of new agricultural technology in farm production has also transformed the farm economy and the mode of life. The family, class and institutional life of the tribal communities have been undergoing drastic changes as a result of rapid transformation of the agrarian tribal society to a market based profit oriented, commercial agrarian tribal society. The introduction of parliamentary democracy and adult franchise has made tribal villages even more fully integrated with the wider political system. They are now not only the elected members of local bodies like Gram Panchayat but also members of the state legislature and parliament.[5]

Considering occupational patterns, tribals can be divided into four main groups: settled peasants living close to forests and using forest resources occasionally; practising settled cultivation and also using forest resources; pastoral and nomadic communities; and shifting cultivators.[6] The general trend of inter-occupational mobility was from shifting cultivation to settled agriculture. But the tribals also experienced reverse mobilisation. This shifting of occupation took place whenever the developed communities who in course of time migrated to the tribal areas threatened their settlements. Traditionally, tribals were very prudent in management of resources, land was communitarian and sale of land to outsiders was almost not allowed. But the migrants being developed and with the support of the state, managed to grab tribal land through various unscrupulous methods involving rent and usurious credit.

Historically farming, hunting and gathering tribals have undergone a substantial occupational change in the modern times. Literature on tribal economy suggest that the traditionally farming tribals have been turned into daily wage labourers owing to various factors. Most economic analysts welcomed the shift in occupation. The rationale is that "since the agricultural sector, in general, is universally acknowledged to exhibit the lowest income of all the sectors, it is presumed that a transfer of labour force from agriculture to other sectors or a faster growth of the latter can be interpreted as an improvement."[7]

The scheduled tribe population of West Bengal have diverse occupational pattern. The economic standing of each of the tribal community depends on the occupation its members are involved in suggesting a hierarchy of occupations for the tribals. Throughout India agriculture seems to be the predominant occupation of the tribals followed by agricultural labour. Due to loss of productivity of land, alienation of agricultural land and population pressure, the tribals are forced to shift from their primary occupation to secondary occupations. This shift is not related to the generally constructed theory that a shift from primary to secondary occupation is always a sign of development. One of the major shifts in the occupation pattern of the tribals of West Bengal has been from agricultural land to unorganised sectors of income generating activity.

Industrialisation and Occupational Change among the Tribals

Industry for the purpose of this analysis has to be delineated to refer to labour intensive activities such as mining and related enterprises. The Eastern part of the country is highly rich in natural mineral resources. Many mines and industries are concentrated here. These mines and many of the heavy industries are contributing to the wealth of the nation but the participation of the tribals is minimal. Whatever participation the tribals have in these establishments is at the lowest level of manual work. The terms and conditions of the employment, more often than not, is exploitative in nature leaving aside the unscrupulous methods used by the non-tribals to exploit the tribals unofficially.

Average Literacy Level of Tribals above 18 Years

Literacy Level	*Numbers in %*
Illiterate	56
Educated under TLC	12
Up to 5	22
Up to 10	10
Graduate and above	Nil

Average Annual Income

Income Level in ₹	*Numbers in %*
Below 5,000	17
5,000 to 10,000	74
10,000 to 20,000	09

Average age for marriage of tribal girls	16 years
Average age for marriage of Tribals Boys	19 Years

The average age of marriage of the tribal boys and the girls suggest the level of tribal ignorance of the legal restrictions on marriage. This is natural given the literacy level of the tribals. The study did not focus on the maternal mortality rate and infant mortality rate but natural outcome of young marriage is high infant mortality and high infant mortality.

Average Landholding

Size of the landholding	*Numbers in %*
Landless	29
Below 1 acre	43
1-2 acres	12
2-3 acres	08
3-4	07
4-5 acres	01

The size of land holding was found to the more in case of Santal tribal population in comparison to other tribal populations. There were marginal variation in the landholding sizes among other tribal communities but such variation is insignificant for any analysis.

Monthly Expenditure Pattern

Item	*Amount Spent in ₹*
Food	800
Education of the Children	10
Medicine	90
Creating Assets	50
Loan repayment	00
Travel	30
Entertainment	2
Wastage (Drinking, Smoking, Gambling)	40
Festivals	30
Average total monthly Expenditure	1052

The expenditure on food has been calculated taking into consideration the price of the rice even if it is produced by the tribal himself. Secondly, the expenses on medicine is higher than what the quantitative data shows. The medical expenses is significantly higher for those who have children below 10 years of age as the frequency of visiting a doctor is higher for those than who do not have children in that age group. It must not be concluded that the adults do not fall sick. But they try to treat themselves with the traditional methods of medicine before deciding to visit a doctor. Apart from price involved in visiting a doctor, the distance to be covered and the time to be lost are major factors in deciding when to visit a doctor. Along with valuables, creating assets for the tribals also mean the utensils they use regularly. Every tribal spends some amount buying now and then some assets though hardly fix any monthly budget for this component. Travel is not a regular expense for the tribals as they prefer to walk significant distance. But travel expenses were found to be high among those who have young children or older/disabled persons. Travel expenses incurred during medical emergencies is also included in this category. Wastage seems to be of higher proportion to the income level of the tribals. In comparison to ₹ 800 spent on food, ₹ 40 may not seem that high but it must be understood that while the expenses on food is for a family of 4.2 persons, the amount spent on drinks, smoke and gambling is accounted for one or two members of the family. Amount spent on festivals has been calculated in reference to the total amount spent annually on fixed community celebrations + if the household has recently organised any matrimonial ceremony.

It must be noticed that the least amount spent is on education. The reason for this is non-availability of educational opportunities in the vicinity to send the ward to school. In cases, where the child does go to school, they are primarily government schools and the students are supported through various schemes that rescues them from bearing the burden of educational expenditure at least up to a certain level of schooling. Two factors were found to be responsible for low educational status among the tribal children. First, Education is not in their scheme of living a life. Second, need of work force for generating sustainable income for the family. The primary reason for dropout of the children from the school by the time they reach 5th standard is that by this time they are considered able bodied and are needed to join the work force of the family. It must be made clear here that among the tribals, Santals were found to be relatively better informed about the advantages of education and the literacy level among the Santals was found to be considerably higher then people of other tribal communities.

Repayment of loan found no place in the expenditure pattern giving false allusions that tribals do not borrow. The fact is in most cases, tribals do not repay the loan by cash. In majority of case the tribals borrow for consumption purposes and the source of such loans is always non-institutional sources such as the local moneylender. Knowing full well that the tribal would never be able to repay the loan by cash the moneylender lends money to the tribals. The loan is often taken and repaid in kind, particularly rice or paddy. Rarely do the tribals borrow hard case unless they have medical emergencies or similar other exigencies. But in all cases non-institutional loans are repaid either through a designated portion of the produce from the land or through human labour. The credit pattern is discussed separately in another chapter. It is important to mention here that there are tribals who have repaid non-institutional loans through cash. This was possible on their part because they migrated to other areas where the income is relatively higher during the local lean season. This not being a regular phenomenon, the tribals chose not to put any figures against their regular expenditures under this head. Secondly, some tribals were found to have availed institutional credit under various credit schemes of the state and the central government but none was found to be bothering about paying back such loans. For the purpose of understanding it must be made clear that in most of the cases of institutional credit the recipient was found to be a Santal and only one case of an Oraon.

If one looks at the average annual income level of the tribals of the district and their monthly expenditure pattern, a clear annual deficiency for most of the tribals. This indicate that the tribals do avail credit from some sources. But interestingly very few respondents admitted of availing loans. Through prolonged discussion with the tribals and local knowledgeable persons, it came to the light that by 'loan' the tribals understand only loans taken from institutional sources such as bank. Seldom do the tribals avail institutional credit facility. This is primarily due to the lesser asset base of the tribals which, in most cases, is not sufficient for availing institutional credit. But there is a clear natural relationship between the asset base of the tribal and his requirement of loan. The lesser the asset[8] base the more the need of loan. Of all those who admitted to have taken loans, 85 per cent belonged to the landless or below 1 acre landholding categories. Secondly, the source of obtaining a loan from is seen to be determined by landholding size and the purpose of the loan. Respondents have a fair asset base opt for institutional sources. In most of the cases, people with fair asset base, opt for loans for non-consumption purposes (most of them ended up spending them on consumption either due to the feeling that they would never have to pay back the loan or they received much lesser amount than what was granted to them making the loan amount unviable for initiating the venture the loan was meant for).

Awareness of the Tribals

Thomas Jefferson once said, "eternal vigilance is the price of liberty." In order to protect the liberty and rights of the individuals, the crucial question is the awareness of the individuals. One may not expect the tribals of the districts to be aware of all the rights and liberties enshrined in the constitution of India for the general citizen and for tribals specifically as there literacy level suggest that. But one can certainly except that the tribals are made aware of their rights by those who are in charge of their welfare, particularly considering their subsistence economic condition which needs continuous support and intervention. The effectiveness of the interventions can only be ensured if the recipients of those interventions are enough aware to take advantage of those interventions. What surprisingly during the survey is that the level of awareness of the population is not only limited but, in many cases the information with the tribals, also was skewed.

Government Programmes

Most of the tribals were found to be ill informed about the government policies aimed at their development. An overwhelming majority of the respondents were aware about the policy of land allocation, possibly hinting at land Reforms. But on the question of being a beneficiary of that scheme most were of the opinion that they have got a paper but not land. This was also confirmed by social workers like Mr. Prashant Rakshit, who has been involved in tribal welfare activities since 1983. According to him, in an over estimation, only 40 per cent of those who have been allotted land are in actual possession of land. Other informed people also endorse this view. The second thing the tribals seem to be fairly aware of is the existence of the Public Distribution System. But the awareness seems to be incomplete as the tribals are not aware of their due share and the prices of the commodities. The tribals opined that most of the time the dealer says that the commodities have not arrived. They never seem to have enquired about the reason of constant failure on the part of the dealer in obtaining commodities. Another that came as a surprise is the confusion among tribals about the Public Distribution System and the local party office of the Communist Party of India Marxist [CPI (M)]. This interesting confusion is because of the fact that most of the relief or developmental grants are disbursed from the local CPI (M) local offices and through the members of that particular political party. Thus it was natural for the tribals to confuse between the political party and the distributive mechanism of the administration.

Government Grievance Redressal Mechanism

Few respondents seemed to be aware of government grievance redressal mechanisms. The preferred destination of the tribals to get their grievances redressed is the traditional village dispute settlement mechanism (locally called *Solo Anna*). This is an assembly of elderly people who decide on case of all natures. Awareness about the Panchayat is there but limited. The perception about the Panchayat is limited to the expectation of some generosity from the Panchayat Pradhan.

Natural Resources

Naturally, tribals were found to be well aware about the local natural (forest) resources available. But they lacked knowledge about the potential of these resources in terms of providing income opportunity to the local tribals. Their knowledge is found to be limited to the use of these resources for meeting their daily food and other marginal requirement. They lacked the knowledge of marketing the local natural resources for increased income.

Educational Opportunities

As evident from the expenditure pattern, education occupies the lest priority in list of livelihood priorities of the tribals. But this does not mean the tribals are totally unaware about education. But their perception about education varied in relation to the distance of the educational facilities the tribals of a particular area can have access to. Most common answer to the question of educational opportunity was, "there is no facility/opportunity for education in the vicinity."

Forest Policy

Being forest dwellers one of the primary necessities for the tribals is to made aware about the forest policies of the government. Only then can the programme of joint forest management can achieve its objective. But the tribals seem to be clueless about the frest policies of the government. It is not expected that the tribals would follow and understand each and every policy of the government related to forest and all its implications. Bu what is expected is the tribals to be made aware of those policies they need to know for their advantage. For example, recently the government has initiated two recent programmes. One, the tribals are to apply to the government stating the land they are in possession for over a period of 5 years to be considered for granting patta against those lands. Two, the tribals have to obtain permission, through an application, for using the forest for various purposes other than trading with heavy timber. But most of the tribals were found to be not aware of these two policies of the government. It is only with the help of some non-governmental organisations that some tribals have been able to apply and obtain the permission at least to use the forest.

Organisation of the Tribals

Among all the tribals, only Santals seemed to be aware of the various tribal organisations that exist at the district and the state levels. But hardly any one was found to be an active member of any such organisation. Tribals lesser in number and scattered in terms of geographical distribution lacked awareness about tribal organisations.

Indigenous Solutions

Given the discussed level of awareness and the socio-economic profile of the tribals no indigenous solution can be expected from them. The only solution they could think of was an expectation that that government could ensure two square meals, a roof to take shelter and some cloths to cover the bodies at times. People of this stratum can be of interest for two reasons for any one including the government. Either the interest is to uplift them from their sub-human condition or use them for one's own benefits. The subsequent chapters deal with both the interests on the tribals.

Notes and References

1. Social Position in Hindu Structure is an ascribed one.
2. Household Assets Holding, Indebtedness,Current Borrowings and Repayments of Social Groups in India (as on 30.06.2002, All-India Debt and Investment Survey NSS 59th Round (January–December 2003), http://mospi.nic.in/rept%20_%20pubn/ftest.asp?rept_id=503&type =nsso.
3. Arup Mahapatra, (2005), *Demographic Perspectives on Indian Tribes*, (Oxford: OUP, p. 53).
4. Data collected from 16 villages of three Blocks of Purulia district.
5. Somnath Mukherjee, Prof. Pranab Kr. Chattopadhaya and Uma Sankar Malik, " Ecological Degradation and the Tribal Livelihood in Purulia – a Backward District of West Bengal", http://www.ecoinsee.org/fbconf/Sub%20Theme%20A/Somnath%20Mukherjee%20.pdf.
6. For a detailed discussion on the Political economy of the tribals, see B.B. Chaudhury, "Adivasi and Aranyaka: Reconsidering Some Characterisations of Their Polity and Economy in Pre-colonial and Colonial India," in B.B. Chaudhury & Arun Bandopadhyay (ed.) (2004),

Tribes, Forest, and Social Formation in Indian History, (New Delhi: Manohar, pp. 89-108).

7. R.S. Singh (1986), *Changing Occupational Structure of Scheduled Tribes*, (New Delhi: Inter India Publications, p. 181).
8. Asset also includes landholding.

III

Politics of Indebtedness

I have learnt to seek my happiness by limiting my desires rather than in attempting to satisfy them.

–John Stuart Mill

I. History of Pauperisation of Tribals

The tribals of India were leading a life of freedom and self-respect in the midst of plenty of land and forest resources with a different socio-cultural milieu till they were invaded by the forces of colonization, industrialization and modernisation.[1] The British brought the tribal India under control with the help of non-tribals. Taking the advantage of the exploitative land, revenue and forest policy of the British Raj the non-tribals emerged as powerful landlords, Zamindars, moneylenders, forest officials and intermediaries of other kinds in the tribal areas.[2] This western district of West Bengal has earned fame for its poverty and of late for militant upsurge. Poverty is conspicuous in the district and so is exploitation of the poor. One has to reflect on the fact that why has there not been a dent to the poverty situation in the district in spite of interventions by the state as well as the central government for over six decades? Several studies have shown that poverty was never new to the indigenous people of this district. For an understanding of the present poverty situation in the district, one has to delve into the past and try to find out the if the relation of the population with the forces of production had any anomaly that has created this present situation of perpetual poverty for some and prosperity for some others.

Agrarian Economy and the Origin of Indebtedness in India

Indebtedness is the most generalised way of living in the world today.

It is a normal mode of everyday existence for individuals in advanced societies where credit cards and personal bank loans are accepted forms of transaction though it involves indebtedness for a certain period of time.[3] But the indebtedness of the indigenous people or the tribals does not fall into the category of affluent indebtedness. Indebtedness for them has become a condition of perpetuity which started with the introduction of money into their world. The tribals who never needed anything from the outside world and produced almost everything for themselves, were introduced to money and market. The introduction of market meant availability of readymade commodities they were producing. Logically, the concept of profit of the trader became the first reason of indebtedness of the tribals. The artificial difference of value included in the price of the commodity was beyond the productive capability of the tribals.

The traditional Indian economy, particularly rural economy has been an agriculture based economy. For the tribals, agriculture was supplemented by forest. But poverty as a concept in India has its origin primarily in the agrarian structure of India. Therefore, one must look at the agrarian system of the traditional Indian society with an intent to find out the causes of inequality and subsequent poverty for a large section of the population.

Prior to the advent of the British, land was under the control of the communities and nominally placed under the custody of the village head. This concept of village head turned into the concept Zamindars. Till that date, there was hardly any problem as the Zamindari system was symbiotic so far as the interaction and dependency of the landlord and the peasants were concerned. Poverty, though was there, was more relative than absolute. The process of perpetual poverty began with the introduction of revenue farming by the British who had neither any understanding of the Indian agrarian system nor did they have any value for Indian social system.[4] D.A. Pundlik observes:

> ... With the advent of British rule in India new forces were introduced which threw the country's economy into the melting pot. The self-sufficiency and solidarity of the village economy disappeared. Cash economy replaced barter. Agriculture began to be commercialised and the land values began to rise with the consequent increase in the credit need of the agriculturist and the inevitable resort to the money-lender.[5]

The single motive behind overthrowing the age-old pattern of agriculture was increasing the revenue form the land that was the desperate need of the East India Company to meet its commercial obligations in England. This led to commercialisation of land and made the income of the peasants uncertain as they were not sure what would be left with them after meeting the fluctuating demands of the revenue farmers. This system of revenue farming was perpetuated through the permanent settlement of 1793. Under this system, the Zamindars were to pay a certain amount to the government and in tern were forced to collect high rent from the tenants through the use of *Regulation VII of 1799*.[6] This was followed by legalisation of intermediate tenures, which made the revenue system multi-tier. The consequence of all these was that the ryots failed to gain much after satisfying the revenue demands of all the levels and thus started sinking in debt. This can be identified as the beginning of the process of indebtedness of the ryots. The concept of intermediate tenures created a class of rent receivers and the exploitative mechanism was set in motion. The ryots often failed to pay the rent owing the high amount of the rent and occasional crop failures causing indebtedness.

Currently, indebtedness seems to be a natural condition of the tribals. The magnitude of indebtedness may vary but it is universal in India. Traditionally, it is assumed that tribals engaged in agriculture are more prone to indebtedness. But there are numerous studies to suggest that tribal indebtedness is not limited to any particular occupation. It is said that "the tribal borrower is born in debt, lives in debt and dies in debt."[7] It is certainly interesting to observe that the tribals throughout the country depend more on non-institutional sources for loans than on institutional sources such as banks and other financial institutions. One reason for the unusual preference is that most of the tribals do not possess the requisite documents to deposit with the institutional financial institutions as collateral. Secondly, most of the tribal loans are unproductive consumption loans for which the formal financial institutions do not extend loans easily. "The credit system in the tribal society includes various kinds of 'Social loans' and 'Economic loans'. From the creditor's point of view, it involves: (i) lending money for interest, (ii) lending money for the sake of returns in kind; (iii) lending money for the sake of labour; (iv) lending loans in kinds for the sake of return with interest in kind."[8]

Most of the earlier researches have traced the reason of indebtedness to the agrarian economic structure of the tribal society.

During the colonial times farmers all over India were reeling under heavy burden of debt. The unfamiliar and unsuitable British policies made rural indebtedness an ever more wide-spread problem. The Central Banking Enquiry Committee of 1931 observed that "on the question whether the volume of agricultural indebtedness is increasing or decreasing, there is a general consensus of opinion that the volume has been increasing in the course of the last century."[9] D.A. Pundlik provides accounts of the increasing indebtedness among the rural poor of the country by the end of the British Raj. He cites Sir Edward Maclegan putting the amount of debt of rural India at 300 crores for 1911 and for 1937 the Agricultural Credit Department of Reserve Bank of India puts the figures at 1,800 crores.[10] Agriculture, during colonial times, was carried out as a mode of living aiming at production of food grains for the family without any commercial objectives. Thus the farmer was in a position to support himself and his family in good harvest years but was at the mercy of the landlord/moneylender during the years of low or bad harvest. This subsistence living of the farmers was further pressurised by visits of famine and flood in tandem. To add to these, the increasing population pressure, fragmentation of landholdings, absence of subsidiary industries helped each other to aggravate the plight of the farmers forcing them into a condition of perpetual poverty. Agriculture no longer seemed to be a viable livelihood option but in the absence of any other option they desperately had to cling to it.[11] The net result is that the subsistence economy of the Tribal turned into deficit economy with increasing indebtedness.

There being no initiatives by the British government to improve the situation of the farmers and in the absence of institutional credit facility for the farmers, the local *Sahukars* (moneylenders) saw a good opportunity to exploit the farmers. The credit pattern was such that the interest rates were arbitrary and usurious. It varied from 150 per cent to 360 per cent in certain cases. Not surprisingly, most of the farmers failed to repay the loans and thus were trapped in the perpetual slavery in the form of bonded labour. The magnitude of indebtedness was as high as 90 per cent of the rural population.[12]

This was the general condition of the farmers all over the country but the relatively isolated tribals were though indebted during the colonial times, the reasons were not the same as in the case of farmers of the plains. The simple reason for this argument is that the tribals, though were dependent on agriculture, had forest to supplement their income from the land and during the times of bad harvest, forest provided all the components of tribal food basket. The process of tribal indebtedness, therefore, was complete with the implementation of Forest Policy of government of India that alienated the tribals from their land and from the forest resources.

It is by no means to suggest that the British Raj did not make any attempt to arrest the problem of rural indebtedness. The Usurious Loans Act 1918, Debt Conciliation Act 1936, Moneylenders Act 1900, Debtors' Protection Act, 1936 were enacted one after the other but these being just legislative measures without any proper implementation strategy failed to make any dent to the indebted conditions of the rural poor. After independence it was assumed that the indebted situation of the farmers would improve. The initiatives the government of India and the state governments have taken to this effect would form the contents of another chapter.

Theoretically, increasing indebtedness is a sign of prosperity and in an agrarian system, indebtedness is conceived as natural and necessary. As the capital of the farmer is locked in the land and the stock, it needs to be temporarily mobilised.[13] But the difference in this so called natural phenomenon and the tribal situation of indebtedness is that the tribals get into the condition of indebtedness that forces them to avail credit not to cover the agricultural gestation period but rather to survive. Thus most of the credit availed by the rural tribals are spent on consumption rather than on production.

Industrialisation and New Forms of Indebtedness

The tribal areas, being rich in natural resources, attracted industries. One of the rationale for establishing industries in the tribal areas is to rectify the economic imbalance between the tribals and the non-tribals. But to the contrary the impoverished tribals were thrown into a state of affairs, which was alien to them both economically and socially. Industrialisation brought with it new values and economic modus operandi that were beyond the comprehension of the simple tribals. The competitive nature of the industrial society brought on unprecedented changes both benevolent and spiteful. Industrialisation of the tribal areas led to modernisation[14] of the tribal belt earlier isolated from the rest of the country but it is debatable whether it served the interest of the tribals and actually modernised the tribals. But one thing is for certain that it did not produce the intended results for the tribals as officially was visualised. There are two views about the impact of industrialisation of the tribal areas. One school of thought regards industrialisation as anti-tribal and another school considers it as an opportunity for the tribals to get socialised into the socio-economic mainstream of the nation.

Industrialisation "refers to the transition in methods of production that has been responsible for the vastly increased wealth creating capacity of modern societies compared with traditional systems. It may refer to manufacturing, agriculture and administration."[15] This inclusive definition of industrialisation is hardly applicable to the process of industrialisation in the tribal areas. The distinctive feature of industrialisation of tribal areas is that it is a process of exclusion of the indigenous population from the process of development of their own locality. Mass displacement of the tribal population from their traditional establishments to alien areas (either to upper hilly areas or to urban areas) making them support less. Numerous studies have indicated that the twin objectives of industrialisation of the tribal areas; i.e. rapid economic growth of the tribal population and cultural exchanges between the tribals and the urban population have been proved to be myths.[16]

II. Income–Expenditure Pattern (Subsistence Income Vs Extravagant Expenditure?)

The average annual income of all tribal groups is between ₹ 5,000 to ₹10,000. This is inclusive of the income from agriculture.[17] In comparison to this the expenditure was certainly higher in normal circumstances. But this never worried the tribals as they traditionally never lived in relation to market economy so that their livelihoods would be affected by pure income expenditure terms. The traditional coping mechanism was provided by the forest from where the tribals could gather enough supplements to support themselves in addition to their meagre income. But in the event of substantial decrease in forest cover the tribals are at the mercy of others. The trouble comes to the tribals when there is some festival that the community has to celebrate or there is some medical emergency. It is an age old idea that tribals live an extravagant lifestyle that put them in condition of shortage every year. True that tribals are serious about the festivals but to conclude that the festivals entail great expenditure is putting the non-tribal paradigm on the tribal life-style. The tribal celebrations traditionally were never beyond the resources at their disposal. It is by means of negative sanskritisation that some element of extravagance has come into their living. Introduction of rituals involving high cost, drinking of pre-made liquor have certainly increased their expenditure during festivals. But interstingly, the tribals do not seem to be complaining about the festivals or related expenses. In the opinion of the villagers the tribals remain ready for the festivities that are to figure at a particular time of the year. They remain vulnerable to two things in their lives; the appearance of guests; and medical emergency. In both cases they are to depend on credit from non-institutional sources. This provides an opportunity to the non-tribals for exploiting the tribals. The credit extended to the tribal attracts unusually high interest and the modes of repayment leads to a kind of voluntary bonded labour. The system of bonded labour is discussed in detail in subsequent section.

Crisis (Getting out and falling again)

Chronic poverty is primarily distinguishable from other forms of poverty by its longevity, with duration of five years being the minimum accepted definition.[18] Recent approaches are helpful in moving beyond the substantial conceptual and practical limitations of an income-only approach. These suggest the need to understand the extent that the causes and dimensions of poverty differ spatially (between regions, rural and urban areas, within villages and households), temporally (according to seasonality and short-term shocks) and according to social structures. The combination of ecological variability, class relations formed around the contestation of resources and social relations embodying gender and caste is particularly significant in the study of chronic poverty, since those who are chronically poor are likely to be in a subordinate position in relation to many of these variables at once. Thus the kinds of social, political and economic conditions that may assist or constrain are likely to be quite different between the chronic and transitorily poor.

Earlier studies have tried to measure the duration of poverty for an individual or a household. The assumption of these studies is that most people are expected to experience a spell of poverty.[19] This assertion cannot be challenged as this can be true for a good number of people. But such studies fail to explain why some people face such spells of time and why some remain in the condition of poverty perpetually. It was found during the study that the tribals of this district are part of an exploitative economic system that keeps them in a condition of perpetual poverty. Their coming out of poverty is in fact a condition of relative lesser poverty in comparison to their conditions of abject poverty.

III. Forms of Exploitation: Land Alienation

There seems to be no change in the situation of the rural poor in the country and particularly the tribals who are increasingly becoming indebted. Indebtedness is probably the most difficult problem faced by the tribal population in India. It is due to rampant poverty, loss of tribal rights over land and forests as well as poor and primitive mode of agriculture, etc. It has not only economic dimensions but also social and political dimensions.

Agriculture is the primary occupation of the tribals. Nearly 88 per cent Scheduled Tribes are engaged in agriculture. Besides, tribals have great emotional attachment with their lands. Their chronic indebtedness to the moneylenders becomes the primary factor in land alienation. Their simplicity and ignorance only accelerate their impoverishment. The other methods that the civilised people use to encroach upon the lands of the tribals are by utilising the intimidation of court, and by using the method of temptation of immediate gain.

Conceptually, the term land alienation of tribals is indicative of the facts that passing of land from tribal to tribal is a simple transaction while the transfer of land from tribal to non-tribal is land alienation. "The term 'land alienation' was coined by the British, who treated others as non-tribals, including themselves as aliens."[20] Historically tribals have been residing in remote forest areas. They developed land and brought it under cultivation and owned land mostly on communitarian principles. The interaction of tribal people with other people and indebtedness of the tribal fold resulted in large-scale alienation of land from the tribals. Though there was exploitation of the tribals earlier, there was no alienation of land from the tribals but the process of land alienation began with the exposure of the tribals to the aliens who entered the tribal areas in the name of national development and tribal development and specifically for industrial development. It would be gross mistake to assume that only aliens exploited the tribals. In some cases the exploiters are within the tribal community itself.[21]

In ancient times the Raja, Maharajas exploited the tribals taking advantage of their uncontaminated faith on the Rajas and Maharajas. Later money-lenders, traders and merchants took over the role of exploiters taking advantage of the poverty and ignorance of the tribals. Things were hoped to change after independence of the country, but some mindless developmental policies of the government and bad implementation of well thought policies by corrupt officials have strengthened the hands of the exploiters by facilitating the process of tribal exploitation leaving them in the condition of perpetual indebtedness.

The British introduced three types of land revenue systems namely: (i) Zamindari; (Mehalwari) and (ii) Ryotwari. Though most of the tribal areas were not touched. The management of tribal lands varied greatly from princely state to princely state. There was hardly any proper recording of tribal lands. Wherever records were prepared they were rough and based on criteria that were insufficient for determination of quantity of land. The net result of improper land record was "that the tribal was not recognised as the owner of the land he occupied and cultivated."[22]

The second reason of land alienation from the tribals was written documents. With the introduction of Land Acquisition Act of 1894 the tribals lost control over their land, which they owned and cultivated commonly for ages. "This incongruous situation has not been rectified anywhere even though its ill effects are quite well known."[23]

After independence and passing of legislations prohibiting transfer of land to non-tribals, theoretically alienation of tribal land has been arrested to some extent. But in the words of Sadhu Singh Srdar a social activist of the district, land alienation was a feature which was prevalent till very recently and is also present in some discrete form in some part of the district and applicable to some tribal communities more than some other communities. According to him the tribals at a point of time owned maximum land in the district being indigenous to the area. But lost to the non-tribals (another respondent, a Santal, terms the non-tribals as Bengalis) through various means adopted by the latter. According to Bholanath, a Sabar, in Radha Nagar a tribal sold a land of 56 decimal of land for a meagre ₹ 450 to Gunjarani Mahatan (A non-tribal lady). But cases of recent alienation of land were found to be rare and almost unreported in terms of personal information shared by the respondents. But cases of tribals mortgaging the produce of their land against periodic loans were still found to be regular in some parts of the district. But the tribal condition has not improved and obtaining loan from non-institutional sources has also not stopped. But the question is who gives them loan and how do the tribals repay the loan. This brings us to the question of bonded labour, another form of tribal exploitation.

Bonded Labour

"Where it is possible for the cultivator to be self-supporting, where land is not in short supply, no voluntary labour will be forthcoming and forced labour in one form or other is inevitable."[24] There are conflicting explanations for the rise and perpetuation of bonded labour but no single explanation is good enough to provide a plausible explanation for the practice of bonded labour in India and particularly involving the tribals. According to the laws of Manu, the practice of bonded labour defined in terms of personal servitude to compensate for interest was illegal in India.[25] The names for the practice of bonded labour vary but the nature of exploitation in all these forms is same or at the least similar and in all cases the victims are those who constitute the lowest rung of the society, i.e. the Scheduled Caste and Scheduled Tribes. Bonded labour continued throughout the British period despite the Slavery Abolition Act of 1843 and in independent India it is still continuing despite the Bonded Labour System (Abolition) Act of 1976.

In the district, as mentioned in an earlier section, the tribals maintain a subsistence life and remain vulnerable for a considerable period of time in a year. They have to depend on the local *sahukar* or moneylender for overriding this critical phase of the year. The system of bonded labour is operated in a veiled form as to give a picture of natural economic relationship in a fairly unequal society. During the field survey it was found that nearly 42 per cent of the respondents resort to take periodic loans from the moneylenders. In almost all cases, the moneylender is a non-tribal. Interaction with the tribals who have availed this kind of loans revealed the entire system of exploitation of the tribals through bonded labour system.

Just one Example

In Bandwan block, there is this famous Aam Jharna village. Situated in a fairly inaccessible place. This is a hamlet of 15 Sabar Families. The example is of Sambhu Sabar. Sambhu has a family of five members, his wife and three children. He owns a rocky land of 30 decimal. Among other assets he owns a bicycle and few poultry. He does not have any qualms about his economic condition as he manages to feed his family from his income from four sources. Meagre income from the land, income from daily wage agricultural activity, selling livestock (poultry), and periodic migration. Early this year, he had borrowed ₹ 400 from a non-tribal (in his own words a Bengali *sahukar* namely Raghupati Beat). This loan he had obtained in two occasions, within a span of one month. Once ₹ 300 when he had guests at home and second when he had to take his third child to the hospital for some treatment. He was effusive in praise of the *Sahukar* who lent him the money when he needed it the most.

Given the condition of Sambhu Sabar, it could be well comprehended that he can never accumulate enough money to repay the borrowed 400 rupees at one time. But he knows how to pay it. He has done it many times earlier. He has to pay through his and his wife's labour. The *sahukar* had made it clear that the loan had an interest of 50 per cent per month (in his on words, *Ek maas por ekso takata dedso holo. Ei bhabe amake 600 taka sodh korte holo*). The loan of ₹ 400 stood at ₹ 600 at the end of a month. This seems usurious but not alarming even if the deal has the clause the for the next month the principal amount would be considered as ₹ 600. Now, being honest to his commitment he tried to repay the loan at the end of one month. The calculation of repayment is interesting. There was no provision in the verbal contract at the time of loan disbursal that Sambhu has to repay through his labour through a fixed price of his or his wife's per day labour. Now when Sambhu approaches the *Sahukar* to repay through his and his wife's labour, the *sahukar* is prompt to say he does not need his labour that essentially now, but if he insists on working for paying back his debt, he can work at a rate lesser the market wage. *Sambhu reveals that the market price for a day's labour is ₹ 30 but the Sahukar said he would pay ₹ 20.* Now one has to calculate the interest of loan when Sambhu finally paid up in full. Though both Sambhu and his wife worked for the repayment of loan. The calculation is made as if only one has worked. If the daily wage is fixed at ₹ 20 per day, Sambhu needs to work for 30 days to pay back the loan in full. But working continuously for 30 days without bringing home any money is not possible for Sambhu. The moneylender is generous enough to understand his plight. He allows Sambhu to work one day to repay the loan and take the wage for the next day. In other words Sambhu brings home ₹ 20 every alternative day till his loan account of ₹ 600 is settled. This means Sambhu had to work for 60 days with the wage rate of ₹ 20 per day. Out of which he took home ₹ 600 and paid back ₹ 600 as his loan repayment.

First thing that comes to mind is what actually was the rate of interest. To Sambhu it remained 50 per cent. But a fair calculation has to be made in reference to the market price of daily labour. As per the government rule the daily minimum wage is ₹ 68 in the district. Thus, his minimum income for a period of 60 days' labour would have been ₹ 4,080, whereas he got ₹ 1,200 of which he paid back the *sahukar* ₹ 600 and retained ₹ 600. Therefore, Sambhu actually paid ₹ 4080 – ₹ 600 = ₹ 3480 against a loan of ₹ 600 at the end of the second month (since both Sambhu and his wife had to work together, they worked for 30 days). Considering that this was the single case for Sambhu for the year, the interest rate for Smbhu was 380 per cent minimum. The rate of interest apart, the way the labour was exploited may not fit into any definition of bonded labour but in all practical senses, this was bonded labour veiled as economic relationship in an unequal but fair society. Not all get job with the local *sahukar* or moneylender. Then the other option to repay the loan is to work else where and bring back the money and repay the loan. This leads to migration which needs to be studied separately to understand the nuances of the process of seasonal migration of the tribals.

Coal Mines and Tribal Exploitation (Feasting on the Golden Opportunity)

One of the useful natural resources found in plenty in Purulia is coal. The north-eastern part of Purulia is rich in coal. The Purulia district sustained two big Collieries. One is at Ranipur and the other is at Parbelia. Other Coalmines are Deoli and Bhamuria. Coal extraction being a labour intensive job promised great fortunes for the tribals of this area but little seems to have changed in the economic and social condition of the tribals, the indigenous people of this locality. It needs to be mentioned here that though there are four official collieries, the unofficial collieries outnumber these by many fold. While the tribals are the main (manual) workers of the collieries both official and non-official, the management is largely in the hands of inward migrants. The remuneration of the coalmine workers is generally enviable but considering the high-risk nature of the work it can be considered as just. Logically, the tribals should be economically sufficient and socially recognised. But unfortunately, and courtesy a well established chain of exploitative mechanisms, the indebted condition of the tribals is not only perpetuated but aggravated to the extent of forcing them to commit *a kind of suicide in order to live*.

The modus operandi as has been found out is both interesting and scandalous. There is a great flow of coalmine workers from the government owned mines to privately owned mines. In normal parlance it is a healthy sign, but once it is learnt that the privately owned mines are illegal, one certainly has to speculate and doubt the process. The miners in the official mines enjoy economic security to cover the risk to their lives and other coverage including health insurance and a decent salary. Then what makes these miners to leave this secured job to join the high-risk illegal mines without any securities whatsoever? It is found that this migration from the government mine to illegal private mine is an *involuntary* act and the instrument used to cause this migration is the well thought "*Voluntary*" retirement scheme.

The complications of the process have its roots in the lifestyle of the tribals. The tribals in this district, as elsewhere, are hardworking, easygoing and always live on the edge without any thought for the future. Given their affinity with nature this caused no major harm to their livelihoods, as they knew the art of making sustainable use of the natural resources and products. The inward immigrants to this region took advantage of this pattern of lifestyle and used the easygoing habit of the tribals to exploit the fruits of their hard labour. Coalmines in the district came as a relief to the already pauperised landless tribals. It is both labour intensive and large-scale activities that promised to provide adequate jobs opportunities to the tribals while satiating the national energy requirements. On the contrary, this actually is serving the out of job moneylenders. The traditional moneylender had lost his job owing the pauperisation of the tribals, but the new job opportunity for the tribals also brought with it the opportunity of exploitation for moneylenders. The combined effort of the government, both colonial and independent, and the inward migrants of the past created the conducive conditions for starting the process of exploitation all over again. The economic might of the inward migrants helped them to establish the dominance of their culture and sanskritised the tribals to a limited extent by exposing the tribals to the external manifestations of the alien culture without allowing them to participate in their economic activities. This increased the expenditure of the tribals by changing their lifestyle, increasing the number of wasteful festivals, and introducing superficial luxuries into the tribal lives.

It is wrong to conclude that these vices were entirely alien to the tribals and was only introduced by the inward migrants. Vices like drinking, festivities were ever present in the tribal culture but they never were that expensive and never included anything that was not available at hand and was extravagant. Drinking comprised liquor made locally from the available grains and fruits and festivities meant drinking and dancing in groups. These changed into *expensive foreign liquor and wasteful expenditure in festivals such as marriages and the like.* The biggest facilitating factor in the process of both traditional and neo forms of exploitations is the high level of ignorance of the tribals. The manual work force of the coalmines comprises mainly ignorant tribals, who are hard working and gullible. The supervisory level (Who come in direct contact of the manual workers) of the coal industry is manned by primarily *second and third* generation aliens. Being habitual moneylenders, they see an opportunity and indulge the innocent tribals in wasteful activities and thus draw them into a trap of indebtedness. This starts by extending small time loans to meet daily expenses such as drinks, tobacco and food. These small time loans are advanced as good gestures towards the ever-needy (artificial needs) tribals, thus does not require any accounting and paperwork. This continues for a considerable period of time. The lenders do not insist on repayment on the salary day initially (probably never). Hell befalls one fine day. The lender generously calculates the loan and the interest accrued on that and informs the tribal of his outstanding.

The amount is such that under no condition can the poor worker repay the amount from his regular monthly salary. The lender does not relent in pressurising the tribal for an early repayment of his money. This is a hapless condition for the poor tribal. Just when the indebted tribal is trying in vain to search for an way to repay the loan, some one approaches him with a ready made solution that would not only repay his loans but also would leave him as free as ever having some cash in hand to live a good life in the future. This beautiful solution is *Golden*, a term used to refer to 'Golden Handshake' or 'Voluntary Retirement'. An excellent idea for the tribal who does not bother about anything but starts dreaming about the apparent good life with cash at the end of the day. Little does he know what is in store for him in the future. The person proposing the idea volunteers to facilitate the process of 'golden' only at the cost of a commission of mere 10-

15 per cent. The process is completed without any fuss and with full consent of the tribal worker. The loan is duly repaid and the commission is paid as promised and what remains (if at all) at hand will support his drinks expenses for a week at the best. The good days are over and the tribal worker is left with no money, no job and needless to say no land which he had already lost. The 'golden' opportunity is well used by the moneylender to feast on the income and social security of the tribal worker. This does not end his exploitation. One would wonder what remains now to be exploited. The answer is his labour and his expertise in extracting coal. Thus, the hardworking tribal is again back to the same job but this time without any security, and risk cover and at a remuneration much less than before.

Ensuring Death: Life Insurance as a Means of Exploitation

Insuring personal life is a sign of modernity. This is thought to be the first act of prudence for anyone involved in income generation activities involving high risk. Thus, learning that the coalmine workers of the district are covered under life insurance is quite satisfying. But a little curiosity is bound to arise, as it seems unusual for the completely ignorant tribals to think in terms of insuring lives. A thorough probe revealed another well-established process of tribal exploitation.

Fear of death is universal and no one can escape this fear only one can prepare for reducing the damages to his family. This is what is the logic of life insurance, except of course tax exemption. The latter is no way applicable to the tribals, as the coalmine workers do not earn enough to fall within the tax net. Given their level of awareness, it is unthinkable that they would think long-term and prepare for possible death. This lack of awareness is generously realised by the moneylenders of the locality. It must be clarified here that the term moneylender may seem to be a misnomer in this case as not all moneylenders operate in the traditional style of lending money against some kind of collateral. The contemporary moneylender has many forms. Insurance agency is one such kind of money lending in this locality. Insurance agents approach the tribal workers and make them aware of the dangers of the activities they are involved in and pursue them to take cover of life insurance that would cost them a little every month but the return in the future would be huge and it goes without saying that in case of death, which is quite probable, the family gets the financial security for the rest of their lives. This sounds very promising rationale to the tribal who meets death almost everyday. Thus, the agreement is arrived at and the premium is made deductible from the monthly salary of the insured. The same person, in some cases the other than the insurance agent, goes on extending small loans from time to time to meet regular expenses. When, according to the insurance agent or the moneylender, the loan and the interest thereon crosses the paying capacity of the tribal worker, the worker is asked to repay the entire loan at one go and presses for the recovery even using physical means.

This is big trouble for the tribal worker who had no idea of his accumulating loans. When the tribal surrenders before the moneylender, in most cases the insurance agent, the agent comes up with a plan by which he would be able to repay his loans with interest. He advises to surrender the Insurance Policy premature. The immediate problem is certainly solved as the money obtained from the surrender of the Insurance policy helps him to rid over the loan but leaves him with no cover on his life. The money lost due to premature surrender of the policy is a straight loss to the tribal. In combination with the loss of job from the government controlled mine and the loss of Insurance cover is the extreme condition the tribal can ever face and thus forces him to work in the illegal mines controlled by the traditional moneylenders at a wage much less and conditions much worse than before. This process is continued till the tribal can work and earn. It is found that in most cases the two processes of losing the job and the insurance cover happens simultaneously.

It is interesting that the moneylenders never face any kind of resistance from the tribals and never lodge any complain with the authorities. Initially, this came as a surprise but it was not difficult to discover the chain of exploitation that involves almost every one.

IV. Tribal Education: Organised Deprivation

During the colonial period, no attention was paid to the tribal education, as the main aim of the education policy during this period was to create a class of clerks to assist the British government in its administration of this country. After independence the government tried to focus the underprivileged sections of the society namely; the scheduled caste and the scheduled tribal population. "Programmes of free and compulsory education were vigorously implemented.

The level of education of tribals is very low. In spite of the educational policies and programmes, there is no significant change in the literacy rate. According to 2001 census, the tribal literacy rate in India stands at 47.10 per cent.[26] The reasons for the low literacy among the tribals are many but one of the reasons, never highlighted, is the deliberate effort of the non-tribals who have populated the tribal areas to keep the tribals ignorant in the anticipation that increased level of awareness among the tribals will be detrimental to the interest of the ruling class, the non-tribals. Traditionally, the Hindu Shastra does not allow people from all social groups to have access to education. To retain the monopoly of the Brahmins over education, they built educational institutions in exclusive places like "*agraharams, chavadis* or temples" when the Britishers tried to open the education system open to all.[27] This Brahminical tradition is being perpetuated under the veil of modern education. The literacy rate has been increasing steadily over the years but the gap between the scheduled tribes and the general population is also widening. The gap is higher in Gujarat, Maharastra, Orissa and West Bengal.[28] The rate of drop out is the highest among the tribals. At the national level, the rate of enrolment is lowest and the drop out rate is the highest among the tribal students. The national drop out average is 10.64 per cent[29] but the average for Scheduled Tribe students is as high as 63.81 per cent at the primary level.[30]

The reasons for such high drop-out of the ST students can be accounted to many factors. Parental attitude, economic background, curriculum and the teaching environment have direct relevance to drop-out of ST students. One wonders that even after sixty years of independence the state could not put its educational policy in perspective to ensure education for all. "One may feel that our education policy makers and planners have shown complacency in assigning due place to educational programmes and in devising appropriate strategies for implementing the same for the benefit of the masses."[31] Another plausible argument for the low literacy among the tribals is the deliberate attempt of the ruling class to keep the tribals ignorant so that the rule of the alien can be perpetuated. It is hard to find information to substantiate this argument but there are sufficient indications towards this. Dr. B.R. Ambedkar discovered the reasons for systematic deprivation. He observed that Brahmins wanted to retain the monopoly over education to misguide and mislead the whole society.[32] During field investigation, it was clear that availability of educational opportunities at accessible proximity is one of the primary determinants for tribals deciding to send their children to educational institutions.

The entire discussion shows that those who are in positions of authority in the administrative, political and social hierarchy have made good use of such positions to keep the exploitative mechanism oiled. The plight of the poor tribals is the source of their wealth thus, it is natural that people in positions of dominance will not harm their own source of prosperity rather would make every effort to enlarge the size of the source. During the survey of the district various interesting facts came out. The drop-out rate among the tribals covered by the study roughly corresponds to the national average of tribal student drop-out. Interestingly, all assessments of educational situation of any region is always based on the situation of the primary education. The higher education seldom is taken into account to make a sense of the education scenario of the district. There are 15 colleges inclusive of technical education. One may consider this number as adequate for a district like Purulia. Being part of the higher education system of the district, I have gained some understanding that will make one's understanding of the educational system of the district complete. As discussed earlier, the district has two categories of population such as the tribals who are indigenous to the district and the non-tribals who are either Bengalis or non-Bengalis who came into the district as inward migrants.

The higher educational institutes of the district have certainly been created to cater to the academic requirements of the people of the district. But in closer scrutiny it would reveal that the educational system is so managed to ensure the exclusion of poor tribal students of the district. As an example one can cite the high admission fees demanded by the colleges is the first hindrance for the tribals which most of the tribal students fail to negotiate. Secondly the demand of capitation fees for honours subjects in colleges acts as another impediment for the tribal students to get quality education. Apart from these official ways to keep the tribals, there are other means to exploit the tribals through the process of imparting higher education. Most of the teachers in these colleges are, in a way, inward migrants to the district. The students are lured and even forced to take tuitions from the teachers. It has come to be seen that during school hours teachers impart private tuitions to students outside the educational institute and even at times within the institute. This illegal and immoral act prevents students from getting quality education from the educational institutes and students are exploited through private tutors who are most often than not the same teachers who are employed to impart education to the tribal students. The ultimate result is that the tribal students are prevented from entering the colleges. Those who manage to enter the institutions of higher education are exploited through immoral business of tuitions.

Thus, it can be argued that there is a process set in place that ensures the exclusion of the tribals from the developmental process of the district. On the other hand the process of authoritative allocation of values acts negatively for the tribals and leaves them at the hands of the non-tribals to be exploited in every possible manner. This process of exploitation creates the condition which does not allow the tribals to get out of the condition of poverty and indebtedness. Now one wonders how the tribals survive this process of continuous exploitation in the hands of the aliens (non-tribals). During the study a major thing came to the fore regarding the coping mechanism of the tribals. It is seasonal migration. The next session reproduces a very informative study conducted by a non-governmental organisation called *Sebabrata.*

Migration in the Context of Tribals of Purulia[33]

Although panel data on seasonal migration in India are lacking, a growing number of micro-studies have established that seasonal migration for employment is growing both in terms of absolute numbers but also in relation to the size of the working population as a whole.[34] The National Commission on Rural Labour (NCRL) puts the number of circular migrants in rural areas alone at around 10 million (including roughly 4.5 million inter-State migrants and 6 million intra-State migrants). But the departments of rural development, agriculture and labour are not geared to dealing with migrants and just regard them as external to the systems that they work with. According to the NCRL, the majority of seasonal migrants are employed in cultivation and plantations, brick-kilns, quarries, construction sites and fish processing. Further, large numbers of seasonal migrants work in urban informal manufacturing, construction, services or transport sectors, employed as casual labourers, head-loaders, rickshaw pullers and hawkers.[35]

However, official awareness of the magnitude of seasonal migration or the importance of it in the lives of the poor is abysmally low. There is little by way of organized accessible support for poor migrants who face insecurity in their source location as well as destination. It is amply made clear by many studies that people prefer to stay at home and the focus of all developmental initiatives has been to make staying at home and working in the locality attractive to reduce the chances of migration.[36]

Seasonal and circular (also known as cyclical, oscillatory) migration has long been part of the livelihood portfolio of poor people across India. It is now recognized that migration is a part of the normal livelihood strategy of the poor and does not occur only during times of emergency or distress. Migration is not essentially a bad economic phenomenon. History is evident of migration of human beings from one place to another in search of better economic opportunities. Therefore, talking about migration in the context of tribal poverty may seem to be a misnomer. But migration does not have equal significance for all migrants. Not always do people migrate in search of prosperity, rather people migrate more out of poverty than in search of prosperity. This is certainly true for the tribals of India and the tribals of Purulia are no exception to this trend. It came as no surprise when it was learnt that during the lean agricultural period, thousands of people leave the district to the near by district head quarters and to other states in search of livelihoods. The most frequented destinations of these jobless tribals include, Burdwan, Durgapur, Dhanbad and even Gujarat. The duration of the migration is three to four months. This seasonal migration has many backward and forward negative linkages that are related to the problems of the tribals and accentuates their problem in geometric progression.

The data below synthesizes 4 months of primary data collected across 10 villages in Manbazar II block of Purulia district.[37] Each of the ten villages, information has been collected from landless, small & marginal, big farmers. There are some differences in the actual variables across the data sets but the results are broadly comparable. Then a broad picture of who migrates, by income, class, caste and gender is prepared. This is followed by a description of specific migration streams in more detail and contains case studies of accumulative and coping migration from the villages to illustrate the complexity of migration and its determinants.

The Magnitude of Migration

Census data[38] collected from 90 households in Manbazar II block of

Purulia district show that migration occurred from all 9 villages, but to varying degrees. On average 75 per cent of the households had at least one member migrating. Recall suggests that the magnitude of migration has grown over time both in terms of the numbers of absolute people migrating and in terms of its importance as a source of household income. But in the absence of baseline data, it is difficult to quantify this increase.

As expected, migration rates were extremely high from villages, which were remote and located in dry areas without assured irrigation and prolonged drought conditions. But as it will be seen in the following section, these figures masked the fact that quite a lot of this migration from drought-prone areas was along old and established routes, which although precipitated due to a 'push' of some kind (such as drought and crop failure) have now become regular and accumulative paths to engaging in high-return labour markets.

Incidence of Migration in Manbazar II Sample Villages

Name of the village	*Total number of households*	*Proportion of households with at least one member migrating (%)*
Tilabani	119	48
Rampur	116	35
Basantapur	227	65
Chaukan	226	57
Dighi	304	55
Bari	237	52
Ankro	710	45
Barmamro	209	35
Dharampur	314	49

Source: Village level interview conducted by Sebabrata.

The highest rates of migration were seen in the case of Basantapur village, where 65 per cent of households had at least one member migrating. This village is located in a very dry and very backward part of the Purulia district. It is nestled in a cluster of villages, all of which are known for their high rates of out-migration to the Burdwan district of West Bengal, agriculturally advanced district. Dry land agriculture is the mainstay of the economy in Basantapur and there are few opportunities outside casual labouring. The average number of days of work available for an agricultural labourer is a mere 35 in the *Kharif* season. Basantapur also had the highest number of persons migrating from each household at 3, suggesting that there are households where nearly everyone migrates. Next was Chaukan, also located in a low potential area where the average number of people migrating per household was 2.

The Returns from Migration

Income from farm and non-farm work inside and outside the village

Seasonal migration as a livelihood strategy appears to be far more important, in terms of returns. Data for the villages studied on average returns per household per annum show that the returns from work outside the village accounted for nearly a fourth of the total (average) income.

In all the villages surveyed, returns were mainly from agricultural labouring, compared to non-farm labouring work. Examining the data by village shows that earnings inside the village were highest in the case of Rampur. The lowest returns from in-village work were seen in Tilabani and Bari, where there are limited opportunities available locally in the farm sector. These villages are drought-prone and backward with hardly any diversification at all. These had the highest average earnings from outside sources, indicating that migration was the main source of earning through both farm and non-farm work. A large proportion of these returns were through high-return agricultural work. Next in rank was Dighi village, a drought-prone. Here, non-farm earnings outside the village were highest. This was largely due to several households in that village engaging in high-return earthwork.

Average Returns Per Household Per Annum (₹)

Village	*Inside the village*			*Outside the village*		
	Farm	*Non-farm*	*Total*	*Farm*	*Non-farm*	*Total*
Tilabani	750	150	900	2500	500	2900
Rampur	1800	300	2100	2000	400	2400
Basantapur	750	300	1050	2100	250	2350
Chaukan	1500	350	1850	1900	500	2400
Dighi	1000	400	1400	2000	500	2500
Bari	750	250	1000	2500	500	2900
Ankro	750	300	1050	1200	300	1500
Barmamro	750	300	1050	2000	600	2600
Dharampur	900	300	1200	1500	500	2000

Source: Village survey conducted by Sebabrata.

As stated earlier, earnings from outside the Tilabani and Bari villages were more than earnings from inside the village and accounted for over half the total (average) earnings. Returns from inside the village were highest in the case of Rampur. The lowest returns from in-village work were seen in Tilabani, where there are limited opportunities available locally both in the farm and non-farm sector due to low irrigation, low capitalization and poor market access. Average earnings outside the village were also highest in the case of Tilabani and Bari, indicating that migration was the main source of earning for these villages through both farm and non-farm work. A large proportion of these returns were through farm sector work, which were coping activities in many cases but had become accumulative for those who had been in the business for longer and acquired skills and contacts. Next in rank were Barmamro, Dighi and Rampur, where farm earnings outside the village were high.

Since employment through agriculture is the most important source of livelihoods for poor labourers, the data on agricultural income is analysed in some detail below.

The returns from agricultural labouring work inside and outside the village

In the study villages, households earn roughly thrice the agricultural income outside the village compared to within. Of the in-village component, *Kharif* earnings are 1.5 times more than *Rabi* earnings. This could be due to the high labour requirements of paddy, which is the main *Kharif* crop. This trend is seen in most of the villages.

Agricultural Labour Incomes Inside and Outside the Village (₹)

Name of the village	*Kharif*	*Rabi*	*Inside total*	*Kharif*	*Rabi*	*Outside total*	*Total income*
Tilabani	480	250	730	1400	700	2100	2830
Rampur	600	200	800	1800	990	2790	3590
Basantapur	750	600	1350	1600	800	1800	2700
Chaukan	600	400	1000	1800	700	2500	3500
Dighi	700	400	1100	2500	420	1320	2070
Bari	550	200	750	1000	500	1500	2250
Ankro	600	300	900	1000	800	2400	3750
Barmamro	500	250	750	900	1000	3500	4600
Dharampur	600	200	800	800	400	1200	2000

Source: Village households' survey Conducted be Sebabrata.

Outside the village, the returns from agricultural labour are nearly two times higher in *Kharif* compared to *Rabi* across all villages.

In all the study villages, in-village per household agricultural labouring incomes is highest in the villages with the highest agricultural productivity and output. These are Basantapur and Dighi. Incomes from outside-village agricultural labour are highest in Barmamro, Ankro and Rampur. These are all agriculturally backward (low irrigation, low capitalization), remote villages with plenty of marginal farmers, more fragmented land holdings and overall less labour opportunities within the village.

Agricultural Labour Income Inside and Outside the Village by Land Category

Land category	*Kharif*	*Rabi*	*Inside total*	*Kharif*	*Rabi*	*Outside total*	*Total income*
Marginal	780	–	780	1500	600	2100	2880
Small	1050	550	1600	1600	450	2050	3650
Medium	250	–	250	1300	900	2200	2450
Landless	1500	500	2000	3500	1200	4700	6700

Source: Household survey conducted by Sebabrata.

In the study villages, the landless derive the highest income from agricultural labour outside the village compared to other classes. The earnings for the landless from outside the village sources are nearly three times as much as in-village. Because of under employment in the villages, they need to search outside.

Who migrates and Why?

It was found that households with more land and assets are less likely to migrate, and that larger households with a higher inverse dependency ratio more likely to migrate. The focus group discussion for the villages shows that there is a significant negative relationship between land owned and migration, i.e. the more the land owned the less the household is likely to migrate.

With regards to livestock, the results show a significant negative relationship, i.e. those with more animals are less likely to migrate. But qualitative information counters these findings, because there are hardly any kinds of migration in the sample villages that depend on livestock. In fact, migration makes it difficult to keep livestock.

Higher migration among the Scheduled Tribes and Scheduled Caste

The FGD shows that, the Scheduled Tribes are several times more likely to migrate compared to upper castes, followed closely by the SCs who are roughly five and a half times more likely to migrate than GCs, and then by Other Backward Castes (OBCs) who are four to four and a half times more likely to migrate. Caste characteristics of migration streams are closely associated with village characteristics and the two reinforce each other, leading to a higher incidence of migration amongst certain castes.

Gender

Much of the literature on migration suggests that it is predominantly men who migrate. But in the study villages, household members were found to migrate in various combinations – men only, women only, men and women, men, women and children. There are marked differences in the gender composition of migration amongst the villages. In almost all the villages, the majority of migrants were male in all villages, whereas in tribal villages such as Basantapur, Chaukan had more female migrants. Even within villages, some streams had more men migrating whereas others had more women. The reasons for this are complex and related to whether or not the skills are gendered, cultural norms to do with women's work and restrictions on women migrating.

The gender possibilities for migration are also determined by caste. For higher caste families it was traditionally often shameful for the woman to work outside her home. There are strong cultural restrictions among the OBC (Mahato) on females working outsides the villages. Therefore, only men from that community migrate for agricultural labouring work. While female participation in labour markets is now widespread, it is still seen as shameful for a woman to leave her own village to work. Lower castes have much less such social pressure. Those with spare labour capacity are able to take advantage of these opportunities create the extra income that can move a household from a deficit to a surplus trajectory.

As a rule, men-only migration occurred where men possess the required skills or in the early years when the activity is relatively new for the community and the destination areas/work are perceived to be too risky to take women and children along. As the migration stream becomes more established and the working arrangements more predictable, women accompany their husbands or may even start going without them.

Gender Profiles of Migrating Households

Village	*Male*	*Female*	*Total*	*% of males in total migrating individuals*	*% of females in total migrating individuals*
Tilabani	110	85	195	77.5	69
Rampur	110	68	168	64	50
Basantapur	250	200	450	79	80
Chaukan	215	150	365	75	78
Dighi	200	150	350	65	60
Bari	190	200	390	72	68
Ankro	450	290	740	69	65
Barmamro	210	150	360	73	69
Dharampur	290	180	470	72	66

Source: Household survey conducted by Sebabrata.

Accumulative and Coping Migration Streams

A common element in the history of migration in all the locations is the way in which it began – usually as a consequence of the push created by a lack of employment opportunities at home and the pull from work availability elsewhere. But different migration streams have evolved differently for different groups of people.

As a rule, the older, better-established migration streams offer high-returns and predictable employment for migrants. These are often streams where stable relations with employers have been built up by particular castes and communities over a long period of time; where specialized skills (often caste-based) are possessed or have been acquired; or where other assets that are needed for migration are available.

In the study villages, examples are long-established farm migration work in Burdwan district of West Bengal. This includes Agricultural labouring in the villages of Burdwan with high productivity, irrigated paddy and vegetable areas, have also become secure sources of income each year that are often able to contribute towards savings or major expenditures. In such cases it is often the dependability that contributes towards the possibilities for accumulation, as time spent searching for work or, even worse, being cheated for work done, is a large opportunity cost.

These kinds of accumulative migration streams have now become a major source of income for many erstwhile poor communities in Purulia and have negligibly contributed to improving their lives through more investment in their farms, houses, health and marriages.

In addition to that, there are more negative kinds of migration streams, which involve a more opportunistic search for work. Often, there is no stable relationship with any particular employer. This happens either when the migrants are relatively new, poor and unskilled or when traditional forms of discrimination work against them so that they may never graduate into better-paid work. In the study villages, this is seen in the case of ST migrants working on brick kilns, who, although working side-by-side with the local, earn only two-thirds as much as them. Even though they live in areas which Government claims having enough work, they do not get enough work during the peak seasons to tide them over the lean season and are forced to migrate for part of the year. Wages can be reasonable, but work is not available every day. Indeed labouring groups in need of work often wait for days on the basis of rumours of work only to discover that the work is non-existent, no longer available or that there are many more people waiting before them. Even if they get work, there is often no guarantee of payment.

Seven migration streams from the study villages were discovered, most of which have not been documented before. Table 14 below provides summary information on the different streams. This information was collected through Focus Group Discussions, Key Informant Interviews and Participant Observation by Block Coordinators who were engaged in the villages for the entire duration of the study. As the table shows, there can be more than one completely distinct type of migration stream or 'option' from the same village. Some of these are treated in detail in the text in order to highlight the major accumulative and coping streams.

Findings

The main findings from this study are summarized in the following points:

- A large cost in migration is the search cost and moral hazard of being cheated. Migration options become more and more secure, and thus attractive, over time. For those who have

Coping and accumulative migration streams in the villages studied

Village name and characteristics	*Caste, skill and asset base of migrants*	*Type of work and when*	*Who migrates*	*Source, amount and purpose of credit/advance*	*Coping or accumulative and wage rate*	*Impact on migrant household and source location*
Dighi village – Far from urban centre with poor transport links, Unirrigated agriculture.	ST and OBC – skilled earth workers, small and marginal farmers.	Agricultural labour works. Migrate during non–rainy season.	Able–bodied men and sometimes their wives. New/young families: all members migrate. In older/larger families couples take turns so that others can care for livestock, farm and children.	Middleman pays for one way, transport and shelter at the landowners' area. Weekly payment made in kind (rice), cash payment at the end of the work.	Accumulative and always has been. Averages Rs 45/day.	Increase in wage income compared to that of in the village.
Ankro village	ST – marginal farmers.	Work in the villages of Burdwan district. Migrate during lean months.	Able–bodied men. Women migrate because of household economic situation is very bad.	Middleman pays for one way, transport and shelter at the landowners' area. Weekly payment made in kind (rice), cash payment at the end of the work.	Coping when no work at home. Rs 55/day. Work availability low.	Manage to survive during the lean season and drought.
Bari – dry, partly tank irrigated. Comparatively	Mixed.	Non–farm and farm labouring in nearby urban	Both male and female from household.	Middleman pays for one way, transport and shelter at the	Accumulative. Average earning is Rs 50/- day.	Better paid than local casual labouring.

Village name and characteristics	*Caste, skill and asset base of migrants*	*Type of work and when*	*Who migrates*	*Source, amount and purpose of credit/advance*	*Coping or accumulative and wage rate*	*Impact on migrant household and source location*
near district capital.		and Burdwan district villages with irrigated farming. Migrate for 15–30 days at a time.		landowners' area. Weekly payment made in kind (rice), cash payment at the end of the work.		
Dharampur – remote, unirrigated Very large number of marginal and sub marginal holdings. Much of the land is unproductive.	SC and ST. Small and marginal farmers.	Work usually from October–March. In Burdwan district.	Two–three adults from a household migrate (usually two males and one female), together with children.	Employer in destination (he comes or they go in advance of the migration season).	Accumulative now, started as coping migration earlier. Migrants can save up to Rs 3000 after meeting expenses. Most families return with a saving of at least Rs 5,000 in a season	More income but children's education suffers.
Barmamro – remote, unirrigated. Very large number of marginal and sub marginal holdings. Much of the land is unproductive.	SC, St and OBC – poor , marginal farmers.	Burdwan district	Young men, women and breastfeeding children.	Middleman pays for one way, transport and shelter at the landowners' area. Weekly payment made in kind (rice), cash payment at the end of the work.	Coping. Rs 60/day when they get work but this is not every day. For those families that have been doing this for several decades and have acquired skills/contacts, the work may be more	Survival in the off–season.

Village name and characteristics	*Caste, skill and asset base of migrants*	*Type of work and when*	*Who migrates*	*Source, amount and purpose of credit/advance*	*Coping or accumulative and wage rate*	*Impact on migrant household and source location*
					regular and therefore accumulative.	
Rampur: Un – irrigated, very large proportion of marginal households.	SC and ST	Agricultural labour in Burdwan districts. Only for 25 days in a year when there is no work locally.	Able–bodied men and women, sometimes children.	Middleman pays for one way, transport and shelter at the landowners' area. Weekly payment made in kind (rice), cash payment at the end of the work.	Coping. Rs 40/day and 2 kg of rice.	Without this work they would have to borrow money.
Basantapur – Undulating with limited agricultural development. 10 kms off main road, restricted access and transport.	Majority ST and SC migrate.	Main migration is in February to April, though some go in November.	Families migrate in groups via middleman (Munim) and often to landlords with whom they have a long–term relationship. Sometimes groups of related single women may migrate.	Munim pays food, and transport one way.	Labour work means that returns can be higher if whole family works together. Accumulative compared to other works. Wages in grain are approx equivalent Rs20/day/person.	Families can save up to Rs 30/day/family. If they get two weeks' work, they can save up to Rs 800. Secures some food security. Involves children, so has impact on schooling..

Source: Focus Group Discussions, Key Informant Interviews and Participant Observation by the study team of *Sebabrata.*

risked going to find new opportunities, and have maintained the link, the investment often pays off.

- Migration is increasingly opening up to women, particularly those from lower castes. Often the woman working as well as the man can make the difference between surplus and deficit.
- Non-farm work is often better paid, but conditions are poor. The work is hard, and is often taken up in the hot summer when agricultural labour markets are slack. Also, because the nature of the work is often transient, there is not the possibility to form longer-term links as with farmers.
- All types of migration can bring new skills. Migration to agriculturally advanced areas for the tribals brought exposure to new forms of green revolution technologies. Likewise, construction work can often bring access to quarter- and semi-skilled work like masonry work.
- The social and domestic trade-offs to migration can be severe. Risk of physical harassment, poor sleeping conditions all brings hazards. If families accompany, then wives, and particularly children, are at great risk from lack of supervision.

We have seen that migration is an integral and regular part of livelihood strategies and production systems; that migration is also undertaken for high-return employment and not only because of shocks and stresses such as drought i.e. that migration can be accumulative or coping; and that migration is a diverse phenomenon with various non-economic determinants including caste and gender. This reflects wider themes with respect to political-economy determinants of access and opportunity. Regardless of whether migration is accumulative or coping, most migrants receive little support and live in very difficult conditions in their destinations. Although their efforts are the real engine of growth in several sectors, providing a cheap and flexible labour source, they remain without an identity and are unable to claim State resources for education, health care, water and sanitation all the time that they are on the move. Women and children suffer the most from this kind of existence.

There are several different positions on what should be done to address the issue of migration. The mainstream view is that migration should be reduced/curbed by creating employment in villages. This is to be achieved through increasing the productivity of dry land agriculture. But it could take several years or even decades for natural resource management and agricultural development programmes to arrest migration. In the meantime, steps need to be taken to support migrants so that their hardships are reduced and they are ensured access to basic needs. Initiative that could be explored through multi-stakeholder consultation is providing migrants with sufficient government's programmes, such as basic healthcare, enrolling their children in the local school so as to avail mid day meal. In addition, ways need to be found to ensure that migrants do not lose their entitlements to PDS rations in their homes.

Although this kind of migration is viewed very positively in terms of its economic impact, it has some negative implications too, particularly for children's education. Smaller and younger families face the greatest hardship because they may not have childcare in the village and must take their children with them. In addition to that, several households lose their access to Public Distribution System (PDS). The dealer claims the rice illegally on their behalf and sells it on the open market.

Living conditions are rough in the destinations. Migrants stay in the field in a makeshift hut. Access to drinking water is difficult and girls are often made to take this responsibility. Similarly, collecting fuel for cooking is difficult. If there is any kind of sickness, labourers depend on private practitioners who are expensive. Social networks are important and migrants help each other in various ways by looking after children and sharing provisions.

Earlier it was mainly the poor and landless who migrated but recently other castes have joined too. It is now common to see one member from a large farmer's household (with more than 10 bighas of land) migrating to Burdwan to supplement their incomes. Rich households use this extra earning to buy household assets including status goods.

Burdwan is the most common destination where they go for agricultural labour work. Most of them leave the village around November and return in June to look after their land. But as droughts in the area have become prolonged, some families are leaving their lands fallow and are more or less permanently away and come back only to celebrate festivals. Half of them take their families along. Both women and men work.

The Primary causes of migration from the district[39]

In a single sentence, the reason for the tribals migrating out can be conclusively said to be poverty of the tribals. A detailed account of the reasons need a repeat of the entire discussion of the themes discussed so far. Thus, it is suffice to say here that subsistence living and lack of assured job opportunity throughout the year forces the people to leave their homelands. This not being a new phenomenon, is being addressed by the government through its various programmes that can be clubbed together as *Food for Work Programme*. The effectiveness of the programme was anticipated even before it was implemented. The then Chief Minister of the state confidently announced that no one would (should) leave the district due to lack of job opportunity. But the figures of exodus during the last two months is indicative of the gravity of the problem of job opportunity in the district. The primary reason for the failure of the programme in preventing mass exodus of the tribals is identified by many, is the process of availing the job opportunity under the National Rural Employment Guarantee Scheme (NREGS). The process is so cumbersome that illiterate tribals find it more convenient to avoid the scheme than availing it. According to the provisions of the scheme the people below poverty line are to enrol themselves under the scheme. The government has to offer job within fifteen days and in the event of non-availability of job the individuals are to again apply. This time if the government fails to provide job opportunity, provision is there to provide unemployment allowance. People below poverty line find it hard to wait for a month to avail the facility of the scheme. Along with the procedural rigidities, corruption at the implementation level ensures its non-fruitfulness in providing work opportunity to the poor. It was notices that the local administration always tries to avoid giving unemployment allowance even if it fails to provide employment opportunity to the poor. In numerous cases the government was found to have provided three says of employment to the poor in a month to make the poor non-eligible for receiving unemployment allowance. Coupled with other problems failed implementation of NREGS leaves the tribals with no other alternative but to leave their homelands in search of livelihoods options for survival.

This process of the seasonal migration has many undesired effects.

1. *Loss of labour force:* The first communitarian effect of the migration of tribals is the loss of labour force to the district.

For a period of three to four months, the district experiences shortage of labour force which affects the economy of the district by reducing the productivity of the district for nearly a quarter of the year. It is pertinent to mention here that Purulia being demographically unsuitable for surplus agriculture, must concentrate on alternative sources of income for the population and for the revenue of the district. But the effort of the government was found to be awfully wanted in creating conditions for creating alternative means of employment. The explanation advanced by the administration for creating alternative employment opportunity in the form industrial development is certainly untenable. Lack of infrastructure is cited as the principal reason or lack of industrial development in most part of the district. There are two arguments that can be advanced as a counter to the argument of lack of infrastructure. Firstly, infrastructure is not a gift of nature that exists in some part of the state and lacks in other parts. Secondly, there are numerous primary industries (mines) in parts of the district. The existence of mimes in some parts of the district shows that exploring mines is not difficult for the industrialists whereas developing forward linking industries is being said to be unfeasible. The logic seems little miss-matched.

2. *Discontinuation of education of children:* The literacy level of the district is relatively lesser in comparison to other districts of the state. The literacy level of the tribals is abysmally lower than other category population of the district. Among the tribals the Sabars are found to be least literate as their literacy percentage is less than 1 per cent. The male literacy is 0.4 per cent and the female literacy is 0.2 per cent. The other tribal groups are in no better position though may be slightly better than the Sabars. Seasonal migration of the entire family for a quarter of the year is one of the important reasons for the tribal children not attending schools.
3. *Inability to create Asset base:* Frequent migration does not allow the tribals to create permanent asset to accumulate. Rather it was revealed by the migrant respondents that they sell their livestock before migrating every time. Or in some cases leave behind at the disposal of neighbours in case the neighbours are also not migrating at the same time.

The end result of migration for the tribals never occurs in increasing their level of income. The unscrupulous means adopted in facilitating their migration indicates the involvement of political forces as well. It was revealed that no matter where the tribals have migrated, if there is an election, all the migrants come (rather brought in trucks) the night before election and go away on the evening of the election day. This shows the connivance of the political forces in the entire process of migration making sure that even desperate measures like migration is not out of the process that ensures the chronic poverty and indebtedness of the tribals. The next chapter discusses the interventions that have been made to alleviate the condition of the tribals.

Notes and References

1. B.B. Mohanty (2003), "Educational Progress of the Scheduled Tribes: A Discursive Review," *Man & Development*, June, p. 91.
2. *Ibid.*
3. Prathama Banerjee (2000), "Debt, time and extravagance: Money and the Making of 'primitives' in colonial Bengal," *The Indian Economic and Social History Review*, vol. 37, no 4, p. 423.
4. Revenue farming was the innovation of the British. It was prevalent in a different form during the Mughal Period. "As a general practice *ijara* or revenue farming pure and simple, lay under official disapproval. Yet in actual fact the revenue officials did sometimes farm out the revenues of the individual villagers ... The revenue farmer was ... not to take anything beyond the equivalent of revenue from the peasants, though there can be little doubt that the farmers would only rarely have respected this injunction." I. Habib (1963), *The Agrarian System of Mughal India, 1550-1707,* (Bombay: Asia Publishing House, pp. 234-235). Cited in the Endnote to Chapter 3, by Manoj Kumar Sanyal (2004), *Peasant Paddy Production Indebtedness and Dispossession,* (New Delhi: Manak Publications, p. 96)
5. D.A. Pundlik (1949), "Thte Problem of Rural Indebtedness," *Rural India*, vol. 12, no. 6, July, p. 289.
6. The regulation VIII of 1799 is also known as *haftam* regulation. The zamindars were assured of all possible assistance from the state machinery in the realisation of rent from the ryots. In case ryots failed, the regulation empowered the zamindars and farmers to attach their crop and even distraint the ryots. See Kabindra Prasad Singh (1987),

Land Revenue Administration in Bihar 1793-1858, (Calcutta: Minerva Associates Publications, p. 72).

7. P. Ramaih and K. Murali Manohar (1992), *Tribal Indebtedness*, (Delhi, Bombay, Nagpur: Himalaya Publishing House, p. 57).
8. *Ibid.*, p. 58.
9. *The Indian Central Banking Committee Report*, 1931, p. 57, cited in R.K. Panda (1985), *Agricultural Indebtedness and Institutional Finance*, (New Delhi: Ashish Publishing House, p. 12).
10. D.A. Pundlik (1949), "The Problem of Rural Indebtedness," *Rural India*, vol. 12, no. 6, July, p. 289.
11. R.K. Panda (1985), *Agricultural Indebtedness and Institutional Finance*, (New Delhi: Ashish Publishing House, p. 13).
12. A.R. Sarat Roy (1939), "Village Vampires: Uproot the Money-lenders," *Rural India*, vol. 1, no. 3, January p. 156.
13. R.K Panda (1985), *Agricultural Indebtedness and Institutional Finance*, New Delhi: Ashish Publishing House, p. 11.
14. Modernisation in this context refers to changes (improvement) in the economic and social structures of the locality not necessarily of the populace of the locality (indigenous).
15. members.ozemail.com.au/~mghslib/subjects/society%20culture/Glossary.htm.
16. Shalina Mehta (1992), Industrialisation of a Tribal Belt: some Observations," *Man in India*, vol. 72, no. 3, pp. 274-275.
17. The Santals were found to be relatively better income generating among the tribals. Their average income could be somewhere around ₹ 15,000 to ₹ 20,000.
18. D. Hulme, Karen Moore (2001), David Shepard Chronic Poverty: meanings and framework CRC Working Paper 2 (Manchester: Chronic Poverty Research Centre, November.
19. Ann Huff Stevens (1999), "Climbing out of Poverty, Falling Back In: Measuring the Persistence of Poverty over Multiple Spells," *The Journal of Human Resources*, vol. 34, no. 3. pp. 557-88.
20. M.L. Patel (1998), *Agrarian Transformation in Tribal India*, New Delhi: M D publications Pvt. Ltd., p. 60.
21. Nandita Singh (1997), "Emerging Problems of Ownership and Exploitation of Communal Land in Tribal Society," *Man in India*, vol. 77, no. 2 & 3, p. 233.
22. R.C. Verma (2003), *Terror by Hunger*, (New Delhi: Aravali Books International (P) Ltd.) p. 32.
23. Johnson Vadakumchery, "The Original Inhabitants of India: Victims of Written Traditions," in Jakes Massey (ed.) (1994), *Indigenous People: Dalit Issues in Theological Debate* (Delhi: ISPCK, p. 127)

24. N.N. Vyas (1980), *Bondage and Exploitation in Tribal India*, (Jaipur, Delhi: Rawat Publications) p. 87.
25. *Ibid.*, p. 89.
26. http://www.nlm.nic.in/lit_scst.htm.
27. P. Radhkrishnana, "Backward Classes in Tamil Nadu: 1872-1988", *EPW*, vol. 25, no. 10, p. 516. Cited by Johnson Vadakumchery, "The Original Inhabitants on India: Victims of Written Traditions, in James Massey (ed.) (1994), Indigenous People: Dalit Issues in Todays Theological Debate (Delhi: ISPCK,) p. 131.
28. B.B. Mohanty (2003), "Educational Progress of the Scheduled Tribes: A Discursive Review," *Man and Development*, June, p. 96.
29. Arun C. Mehta, "Drop-Out Rate at Primary Level: A Note based on Dise 2003-04 & 2004-05 Data," http://scripts.mit.edu/~varun_ag/readinggroup/images/2/21/Dropout.pdf.
30. B.B. Mohanty, "Educational Progress of the Scheduled Tribes: A Discursive Review," *Man and Development*, June 2003, p. 99.
31. Rita Sinha (1996), "Equalization of Educational Opportunities – Scheduled Castes and Scheduled Tribes: Problems and Future Strategies," *Man in India*, vol. 76, no. 2, June, p. 152.
32. B.R. Ambedkar, *Unpublished Writing*, vol. 3, 1987, p. 326 Cited by Johnson Vadakumchery, "The Original Inhabitants on India: Victims of Written Traditions, in James Massey (ed.) (1994), *Indigenous People: Dalit Issues in Today's Theological Debate* (Delhi: ISPCK) p. 131.
33. During the field study I interacted with some NGOs who are working among the tribals. NGO *Sebabrata* is a reputed organization and is famous for conduction research and implementing intervention projects. During my interaction with Mr. Sadhu Singh Sardar, the Secretary of *Sebabrata*, the issue of migration came up as an important coping mechanism the tribals take resort to manage their livelihood. *Sebabrata* was conducting a detailed study on migration of the tribals from the district. I am greatly indebted to *Sebabrata* and to Mr. Sadhu Singh Sardar for sharing their data and interpretation for my use. The entire section on migration is a near representation of *Sebabrata.*
34. Breman, J., Of Peasants, Migrants, and Paupers, Delhi: Oxford University Press, 1985; Breman, J., *Footloose Labour: Working in the Indian Informal Economy,* Cambridge: Cambridge University Press, 1996; Rogaly, B., Biswas, J., Coppard, D., Rafique, A., Rana, K. and Sengupta, A. 'Seasonal Migration, Social Change and Migrants Rights, Lessons from West Bengal', *Economic and Political Weekly*, 8 December: 4547–59.
35. Dev, S.M. (2002), "Pro-poor Growth in India: What do we know about

the Employment Effects of Growth 1980–2000?" Working Paper 161, London: Overseas Development Institute.

36. Farrington, J., Christoplos, I., Kidd, A. with Beckman, M., "Extension, Poverty and Vulnerability: the Scope for Policy Reform: Final Report of a Study Conducted on Behalf of the Neuchâtel Initiative, (2001)" *Working Paper 155*, London: Overseas Development Institute. Rao, U., *Palamoor Labour: A Study of Migrant Labour in Mahabubnagar District*, Hyderabad: C.D. Deshmukh Impact Centre, Council for Social Development, 1994. de Haan, A. Brock, K. and Coulibaly, N. (2002), "Migration, Livelihoods and Institutions: Contrasting Patterns of Migration in Mali," *Journal of Development Studies special issue*.
37. The data was collected for their own study on Migration by Sebabrata, a Non-governmental organization.
38. Basic information on occupation structures, caste, income and asset ownership was collected through a census survey that covered all households in the study villages.
39. Based on the findings of the study conducted by *Sebabrata.* I have drawn the conclusions in for the purpose of my analysis of the politics of indebtednesss.

IV

Interventions: Politics of Development

Poverty has been the single most important bane of developing societies. One of the prime aims of developing countries has been to find effective means to alleviate poverty. There has been optimistic as well as pessimistic assessments of the developmental policies initiated by governments of developing nations. Central to the strategy for alleviating endemic poverty has been improvement in the asset base of the poor.[1]

Nature of Intervention

The first Prime minister of India Pandit Jawaharlal Nehru suggested that the tribals should remain in their tranquil past and no attempt should be made to impose the so-called dominant (modern/civilized) values on them.[2] Though there was some sort of unanimity regarding the need for not over administering the tribal areas as they had traditionally been self-sufficient in their own ways, the need for intervention arose from the demands of national development. Under the planned development approach, it was emphasised that the country, in order to develop must make good use of her natural resources. This requirement of national development forced the Indian state to modify the national approach towards the tribals and thus the state adopted a balanced approach whereby it was aimed to improve the tribal economy while preserving their unique culture and traditions.

One can only wonder why the tribal issue being a high priority issue for the government of independent India has not yielded any positive results. The tribal issue was extensively discussed in the constituent assembly of India and even "the Cabinet Mission's statement of May 16, 1946 clearly mentioned the excluded and the partially excluded areas and the tribal areas as requiring the special attention of the Constituent Assembly."[3] The Constituent Assembly appointed two sub-committees; one on Assam and the other on Excluded and Partially Excluded Areas other than Assam. The two committees in their joint meeting on August 25, 1947 acknowledged that the tribals are being exploited by the non-tribals (plains folks) and alienation of tribal lands through unscrupulous means to non-tribals. The joint meeting further asserted that the tribals have functional village panchayats that greatly help in smothering tribal village administration and replacement of these forms of administration with modern and complicated system of administration would do more harm than good to the tribal societies.[4] The Constituent Assembly spent good amount of time in preparing a scheme for the development of the tribals without affecting their culture and identity. It laid down certain criteria for determining an area as scheduled area that are:

- Preponderance of tribal population;
- Compactness and reasonable size of the area;
- A viable administrative entity such as a district, block or taluk;
- Economic backwardness of the area compared to the neighbouring areas.

Based on these criteria, Purulia does not belong to the category of scheduled area. Thus the plight of the tribals of the non-tribal and non-scheduled areas is much more than their counterparts in the scheduled and tribal areas. However, over the years areas having substantial tribal population have got the attention of the state governments and special schemes have been designed for their development.

The most important of the developmental interventions has been the attempt to improve the terms on which the poor has access to land which is the main source of livelihoods in less developed agrarian economies. Far-reaching Land Reforms have been undertaken in some countries with an intent to transfer property rights to the poor.[5] India is one such country having a large body of legislations on Land Reforms. There are official success stories and apparent failures so far as their implementation and desired results are concerned. Two states of the Indian Union namely Kerala and West Bengal are known for their successful implementation of Land Reforms. The distinctive feature of these states associated with this welfare measure is the rule of the left. Kerala has been under Left Rule in phases whereas the Left Front has ruled West Bengal uninterruptedly since 1977.

The updated Programme of the CPI (M) talking about the tribal people states: "The Adivasi and tribal people who constitute seven crores of the population, are victims of brutal capitalist and semi-feudal exploitation. Their lands are alienated from them, the right to forests denied and they are a source of cheap and bonded labour for the contractors and landlords. In some states there are compact areas inhabited by tribal people who have their own distinct languages and culture. The tribal people have been roused to new consciousness to defend their rights for advancement while preserving their identity and culture. Due to the threat to their identity and very existence and the callous policies of the bourgeois-landlord rulers, separatist tendencies have grown among some sections of the tribal people. Regional autonomy for protecting their rights in the areas which are contiguous and where they are in a majority is a democratic and just demand. The capitalist-landlord-contractor nexus constantly seeks to disrupt their traditional solidarity with some concessions to their leadership, denies their legitimate rights and suppresses them with brutal force".[6]

To meet the demand for land, a central question is to implement land reforms and ensure the distribution of surplus lands to the landless adivasi families. In West Bengal under the Left Front government, 11 lakh acres of surplus land had been distributed to 25 lakh families. Of this, nearly 5 lakh families are tribals.[7]

Land Reforms and the Tribals

The single most important intervention to alleviate the economic condition of the poor in general and the SC and ST in particular has been the land reforms undertaken by various states. The success has varied from state to state but the general observation is that land reforms were a 'complete'[8] success in West Bengal. According to a study conducted by Pranab Bardhan and Dilip Mookherjee[9] there is a negative correlation between Left Front control and successful implementation of land reforms in the state. They have concluded, "Land Reform implementation is the highest in villages where local governments were more evenly contested between Left and the Right Parties."[10] A look at the electoral performance of various parties at the local levels since 1977 shows the complete control of the left parties in the rural areas whereas in urban areas they have faced occasional challenge from other right parties. Dreze, Lanjouw, and Sharma point out that land consolidation on the whole in the state has not been that progressive in its distributive aspect. Richer farmers have used their power to obtain improved holdings.[11]

There has been a constant increase in the number of tenants over the years in the state. Bardhan and Mukherjee presume increased landlessness as the primary reason for such increase. The reasons for increase in landlessness, according to them are, subdivision of families and inward migration of refugees from Bangladesh.[12] The second one is not applicable to Purulia as it has not been that much affected by refugee migration from Bangladesh. But another factor that has substantial contribution in making the farmers landless is land loss caused by un-institutional credit. However, there seems to have been not much impact of land reforms in this district.

Before embarking upon the details of land reforms and its impact on the lives of the tribals of Purulia, it is essential to have an overview of the land tenure system traditionally prevalent in the tribal areas. Before the permanent settlement and before the incoming of the foreigners, the Santhals were in complete control of land in the tribal areas of West Bengal. It was the Santhals who cleared the forest and created cultivable land.[13] The distribution of land was fairly egalitarian as land was divided among the villagers almost equally and rent was collected by the head of the village. Officials in charge of collection of rent enjoyed some rent free land. It was the incoming of the foreigners (dikkus) that resulted in the erosion of this *Mandali* system of land ownership. The informed Bengali and Oriya Mahajans were given permanent *Mokrari lease* by the king for their improvidence.[14] The Mahajans introduced middlemen who were to collect rent and thus the entire system of land alienation began.

The second land tenure system that was the in operation in Purulia was the Ghatwali System. The present Purulia was part of the Jungle Mahal created under the Regulation XVIII of 1805. in the Jungle Mahal, the police administration was placed under the Zamindars. They in turn appointed *Ghatwals* (those responsible for protecting the hill passes from external aggression. For this act every Ghat was created as a unit and placed under the charge of a *Sardar* who in turn appointed *Sadials* who again appointed *Tabedars*. While the Sardar paid a nominal amount (*Panchak*) to the Zamindar as rent. The Sadial pays rent to the Sardar and the Tabedar pays rent to the Sadial. However, after the introduction of permanent settlement, the system continued with slight modification. The entire hierarchy paid their rent directly to the Zamindar who had obtained the lease from the Nagistrate, Collector. This system was abolished later.

The land system that had consolidated itself by the time of India's independence had certain feudal characteristics. The land did not belong to the farmer who was actually tilling the land and there was concentration of land in the hands of the few while a large section of the society remained landless of minimal amount of land that was either unviable cultivation or too little to depend for a substantial period of a year. The government of Independent India contemplated of correcting the anomaly and thus came the famous 'land reforms'. Considering the wide difference in land holding pattern and the nature of land in various parts of the country, land reforms was left the state governments to implement in accordance with the local requirements and conditions.

In the entire country, two states emerged to be really seriously implementing the land reforms programme namely Kerala and West Bengal. In West Bengal, the main thrust of the land reforms programme was the elimination of intermediary interests on land and distribution of surplus lands over ceiling to the landless and land-poor.[15] The objective was not only to redistribute land among the landless but also to provide them with inputs to make the poor self supportive and contribute to the national/state economy. Apart from land redistribution, West Bengal embarked upon another reform measure called 'Operation *Barga*'. Operation *Barga* meant institutionalising sharecropping. For historical reasons sharecropping is prevalent in the state of West Bengal and the state started registering the sharecroppers called *Bargadars*. By registration of the *Bargadars*, the security of tenancy was ensured. Eviction of *Bargadars* was legally prohibited unless the landlord decides to take the land under his possession for self cultivation for economic reasons.

Under the West Bengal land Reforms (Amendment) Act 1972 and other analogous Acts, the tribal population were legally provided protection as transfer of tribal lands to non-tribals was prohibited. According to government of West Bengal claims, as on February 15, 2008, the total quantity of land distributed under land reforms is 1122116 acres and the total number of beneficiaries are 2971857.[16] According to Government of West Bengal, the main beneficiaries of the land redistribution has been the people belonging to the scheduled caste and scheduled tribes. It claims that SC and ST recipients constitute 55 per cent among all the beneficiaries of land redistribution while the presence of SC and ST population to the total population is 28.1 per cent.[17] Secondly, the budget statement 2008-09 claim to have registered 15,10,657 Bargadars as on February 15, 2008.[18]

The land reforms is recognised as a major achievement of the Left Front government and it is said that land reforms is a success in West Bengal. But it seems that land reforms has no effect on the economic condition of the tribals. Measures taken on paper do not reflect on the ground. The ground reality of land reforms in the district under study is entirely different from what the government of the state claims. There have been conflicting interpretations of the impact of land reforms on the economy of the state of West Bengal. Some studies call it a complete success and relate the success to the growth in level of agricultural productivity in the state. The other studies call it a political demonstration without having any substantial impact on the lives of the poor of the state. In this study, the attempt is not to evaluate the impact of land reforms on the economy of the state, rather the focus is to find out how have the tribals (particularly of Purulia district) been benefited from the much talked about land reforms. During field investigation, it was learnt that there are landless tribals still languishing at the bottom of the economic hierarchy of the state. Of the 16 villages covered during the study it was found that the majority of the tribals have below 1 acre of land and to make it clear here that the land under the possession of the tribals has not come through land redistribution under land reforms programme of the Left Front Government of the state. The land of the tribals particularly the Sabars, the most marginalised among the tribals, is accountable to the mobilisation of Sabars by a "*Paschim Banga Kheria Sabar Kalyan Samitii*" a Non-Governmental Organisation. The present land holding of this section of the tribals was once part of the forest that got depleted to satisfy the need and greed of any one except the tribals.

Contrary to the claims of various studies, it was found that Land Reforms cannot have any positive effect on the lives of the tribals of Purulia district. The reasons for such a conclusion are six:

1. Unviable quantity of land
2. land allocated are not fit for cultivation
3. the pattadars were not in actual possession of the land.
4. land were not properly demarcated

5. tribal pattadars are dispossessed by non-tribal or other tribals
6. the patta papers were forcibly taken away by some one else (CPM workers, I was told) from the patta holders

1. Unviable Quantity of Land

The average quantity of land that the tribals have theoretically obtained is less than 0.4 acre. In some cases it was fond that the quantity of land is as minimal as 0.01 acre. This was revealed by the tribals during the field investigation. It must be mentioned here that only those who actually possess the land could give this information. The utter dissatisfaction regarding the quantity of land among the tribals was evident as the tribals were of the opinion that such minimal land served no purpose. On the other hand this land reduced their mobility. The worst affected seemed to be the Sabars who were primarily nomads and earlier changed their place of residence according to requirements in various seasons of the year. Now allocation of land of minimal quantity has forced them to stay fixed at one place and try to cultivate the land however unviable the quantity may be. The quantity of land distributed also figures clearly in a the annexure to the affidavit submitted to Calcutta High Court in 2002 by the then Chief Secretary to the Government of West Bengal Mr. S.N. Roy.[19] According to this document, in some cases, the tribals have been given 5 to 6 plots of land in different place and all are small holdings. The wisdom of the authorities in allocating such miniscule quantity of land must be questioned considering the fact that the geography of Purulia does not permit intensive farming that such small quantity of land can provide support throughout the year.

2. Uncultivable Land

Next to the quantity of the land allocated comes the quality of land. During the travel throughout the three blocks namely Bandwan, Manbazar I and Manbazar II, it was clear that the general quality of land is poor. The land of these blocks are primarily rocky and lack proper irrigation facility. Thus, as such the productivity of the land is poor in comparison to the low laying land of the coastal districts. The authorities cannot be blamed for the nature of land the district has. But it was a surprise to find the way land has been allocated under the famous land reforms programme. Not only the quantity of the land is less the nature of land allocated ensues that the tribals don't get to cultivate the land. What is most surprising is that the divider (*Ail*) between two cultivable lands has been allocated to the tribals as their land. Now it can be imagined that the *Ail* being a marker between two cultivable lands cannot be physically possessed by anyone other than either of the landowners. Secondly, the ridges of canals, river beds, roads were also reported to have been given as land to the tribals under the land reforms programme. Another interesting fact that came to light during field investigation and also found in the government records is that the same plot of land has been allocated to more than one person. In Karu village of Bandwan district a plot of land numbering 1127 has been assigned to as many as six persons. None of the six apparent recipients seems to be in possession. Moreover, for the purpose of livelihoods, the tribals do not bother about this particular plot of land as the same has been identified as unfit for cultivation by the administration itself. By government's own admission, most of the lands distributed among the tribals are not fit for cultivation. In another discovery by the district judge during his enquiry into the condition of the tribals, he discovered that in one case in a 30 decimals of land, 52 Sabars have been granted pattas. However, only one person is in possession of the land.[20]

3. Pattadars not in actual Possession of the Land

Under the land reforms programme, theoretically, land was allotted to the landless and land poor. But in closer scrutiny, it is revealed that those who received land, did so only on paper. This was particularly so in case of tribals. A further classification can also be made within the tribals who lack real possession of land. The Sabars were found to be most discriminated among the tribals who are not in possession of allotted land to them. The reasons for their non-possession of land are many. Firstly, given the level of awareness of the tribals, they are yet to understand that there exist some land in their name. The administration on its part hardly bothered to inform the tribals of the programme of the government which had the objective of allotting land to the landless. The second reason for non-possession of land by the tribals is force used by those who are in position of power and influence to prevent the land, legally vested with the government and subsequently distributed among the landless and the land poor, from being possessed by the tribals who have always depended on the generosity of these influential sections for survival. Thirdly, in some cases, the land allotted to the tribals is being enjoyed by non-tribals on the pretext of charitable use. In numerous instances, the tribals were of the opinion that they have been handed over a piece of paper but do not know where the mentioned land actually is. In some cases, it was reported that non-tribals, mainly people belonging to Mahato community forcibly drive away the tribals when they try to cultivate the land allotted to them on paper. This information from the villagers were found to be true and not hidden from the eyes of the administration as is evident from the report of the district judge of Purulia prepared in 2000 and in the affidavit of the Chief Secretary to the Government of West Bengal submitted to the Calcutta High Court in 2002. In his report, he district judge reveals incriminating evidence against the administration showing total failure of the reach and effectiveness. In Kasidih village there are 20 Sabar families who have received pattas but none of them are in actual possession of the land the judge mentions that "'after one occasion, they have been dispossessed".[21]

4. Land not Properly Demarcated

The most serious flaw in the process of land distribution is lack of demarcation of land. Tribals, traditionally being forest dwellers are not acquainted with land details. But in the event of making an effort to draw them into agriculture, they should be given land not only on paper but also physically. The owner must know which is his land and how much is his land. In the absence of such markings, it had created more confusion and problem for the tribals than any convenience as land related conflicts are increasing in the areas tribals are in majority. The conflict is not only between the tribals and the non-tribals but also among the tribals. It was found that tribals are fighting among themselves on the question of land. It came to light that land which has been under possession of a particular tribal group has been allotted to another tribal group causing severe inter-group conflict. Violent conflicts have erupted in recent past around land possession. The Santhals are numerically superior to other sections of the tribals and thus control most of the resources. And in many a cases they are in conflict with other tribal groups such as Sabars or Mundas on matters of possession of land. Tribals, mainly Sabars complained that they are threatened by Santhals and Mahatos not to cultivate the land allotted to them. It has so happened that the produce of the tribals have at times being taken away by the Mahatos of the locality on the pretext that the land originally belonged to the Mahatos and the law of the land does not seem to command any respect from the Mahatos who are the dominant section throughout the district. In a case detected by the district judge, in Sargo village six Sabars are registered to have received land but none in actual possession of land. Ḿore over, Binode and Chhutulal have got their lands below the river belt. In another case, in Kelardih village, three tribals have been allotted the same plot and the plot itself is a place of worship known as "*Joyer Than*".[22] This has turned into a flash point as the *Joyer Than* is under the control of Santhals and the moment the Sabars who have been allocated the land try to take physical possession of the land, there would be clash between the Sabars and the Santhals.

5. Tribal Pattadars Dispossessed by Non-tribal or other Tribals

In very few cases where the tribals have succeeded in obtaining the papers of the land allotted to them and are in actual possession, there exist another problem. The problem is forcible dispossession of the tribals from their land by the non-tribals. This used to be the regular feature of economic relationship between the tribals and the non-tribals in the past and is known as the process of land alienation discussed in another section of this study. It is suffice here to mention that the land legally redistributed among the landless and the land poor belonged to the non-tribals and some Santhals of the district. Under the land reforms programme the land above the ceiling were vested with the government and were subsequently distributed among the poor. The laws of land reforms do not seem to apply to the cases of tribals as it was revealed that the land legally vested with the government are still being used by the non-tribals who owned them before vesting. In an interesting case authorities are found to have dispossessed the tribals of their land. The land of Sri Sarup Mandi of Kuchia village of Bandwan block has been occupied by the police on the pretext of constructing a camp. The tribals have made repeated complains to the authorities but the case is still not solved and the tribals are not in a position to cultivate the land they owned since 1968.[23] In another case, under Manbazar-I block the legal heirs of a Sabar namely Buddheswar Sabar were dispossessed by three Mahatos. The case was identified by the workers of Paschim Banga Kheria Sabar Kalyan Samiti and the authorities were forced to act and restore possession in the year 2001.[24] But the Sabars remain apprehensive that the Mahatos may any time dispossess them. At Beldih two Sabar lands were taken over by Purulia phosphate without paying any compensation.[25]

6. Patta papers were forcibly taken away by some one else from the patta holders

This is the final reason for academic purposes only as other reasons cannot be ascertained with proof. However, in cases where the tribals have got pattas and have been able to identify their land and tried to cultivate the land they have faced a peculiar problem. The problem is confiscation of the pattas by some one other than those who are entitled to do so. It is needless but must be mentioned that confiscation of patta is not allowed even for any authority without the orders of the judiciary of the country. But it had been reported by the district judge in his report that the pattas have been confiscated by private persons belonging to non-tribal community and in some cases by political authorities who clearly do no have the authority to do so. In Gohmikocha village the pattas of the tribals have been taken away by the Gram Panchayat.[26] In another revelation it came to the notice of the judge that the pattas of the allotted lands have been taken away from the tribals by the ex-pradhan of the Gram Panchayat. During the field investigation it was reported by the tribals that people from the party (CPM) office came and took away the pattas.

The entire discussion of the much acclaimed land reforms programme of the Left Front Government of West Bengal and its impact on the lives of the tribals is testimony of the fact that for the tribals the land reforms programme of the government is nothing but a joke. In other words, this is a big scam that is being termed as a proud achievement of the left front government of West Bengal. Some logical conclusions can safely be drawn about the performance o the political party of the state that stakes claim of being most pro-poor and on that pretext continues to remain in power for more than 30 years by now.

One of the factors identified for the so called success of the land reforms in the state is the presence of large number of cadres of the Left Front at the grass roots levels. These cadres were responsible for identifying surplus land and helped the government in getting these surplus land vested with the government. Secondly, these cadre were again instrumental in identifying the landless and land poor to whom the land was to be distributed. The gross violation of the principles of land reforms and rights of the tribals cannot take place without the involvement and/or knowledge of the left front cadre. According to the responses of the tribal villagers, in most cases those dispossessed the tribals of their allotted land were people belonging to non-tribal communities (particularly the Mahato community) and having substantial political clout in the locality. Thus, a valid conclusion can be made that neither the government not the administration had the actual will to take the land reforms to the tribals and effect changes in their lives. Rather, land reforms was used as a pretext to create a class of cadre who would enjoy the tribal land and remain loyal to the party and the government.

Poverty Alleviation Programmes

It may be a shame but the truth is the tribals lack the three basic necessities of life namely, food, cloth and shelter. If land reforms programme initiated by the Left From Government of West Bengal aimed at ensuring food security for the tribals, "Indira Abas Yojana" was initiated by the central government to provide shelter to the poor. A travel through the tribal areas of Purulia reveals that the tribals are yet to have proper housing that can provide them shelter. A look at the houses would quell some of the misconceptions built around the tribals. It is said that the tribals are responsible for deforestation, but no use of wood is found in the constructions by the tribals. Secondly, some tribals of Purulia, particularly the Sabars were branded as criminal tribe. It can be assumed that criminals can afford to construct a decent house if nothing else. But no house of the Sabars could be found to be built to show any sign of prosperity.

The government of India, as part of its developmental initiative conceptualised a plan to allocate houses for the poor. Tribals, certainly being among the poorest of the poor, were to the beneficiary of this housing project. There is no point in providing the details of the number of houses built under the Indiara Abas Jojana as what matters is the implementation of the programme and the houses being enjoyed by those it was meant for. According to the claims of the government, most of the tribals have been provided with houses under Indiara Abas Jojana but the information from the filed reveals a different picture and the information from the field matches to the findings of other report prepared by the district judge in the year 2000. There seem to have little change between what the Hon'ble judge found during his investigation in 2000 and the present study conducted during the period 2006-08. The condition of the tribal houses is simply inhabitable. The picture above is the representative proof of the house of tribals even today.

Of the 14 villages covered during field investigation, in most villages some tribals have received houses under Indira Abas Yojana. It must be mentioned here that the administration did not identify most of those who have received houses under the scheme. Almost in all cases, the beneficiary was identified by the NGOs working in the locality. It needed constant persuasion by the NGO workers to make the Indira Abas Yojana reach the tribals. The basic reason for the tribals not being able to avail the benefits o the scheme is their ignorance and the non-committal attitude of the administration to reach to the tribals. During the field investigation, not a single house, constructed under the Indira Abas Yojana, was found to be made of bricks. None had concrete roofs as well. All the houses were mud walled and the roof was either, tin or asbestos or tiles. The houses that could be seen during the filed survey were relatively new and constructed recently on the insistence of various NGOs. The longevity of the houses constructed can be questioned from the look of it. The district judge of Purulia in his tour diary has made inflammatory revelations. He has given detailed account of houses collapsing within a year or 15 days of construction. Some of the cases cited by him can be produced as evidence of the callous attitude if not anything else on the part of the administration.[27]

At Makarkendi, the judge found two houses to be existing against the government's claim of 11 houses. At Chirugora, 9 houses were built within 3 to 4 years of time, but all of them collapsed within 15 days of construction. The other houses built under the Indira Abas Yajana were found to be un hygienic and without ventilation. During the field survey this became clear that there has been rampant corruptions in the process of construction of the houses under Indira Abas Yojana. The audit officer has gone on record admitting that bills were passed actually verifying the actual construction of the houses.

Community Development Measures

Dams

Dams, which the local people in their language call Bandh has great significance in the lives of the tribals who are now expected to undertake agriculture as the primary means of livelihood. The topography of the district being uneven and present agricultural land being carved out of earlier hills lack fertility and most importantly lack irrigation facility. Thus, the primary requirement of the tribals initiated into agriculture is availability of water. In other parts of India, it has been seen that people use traditional techniques in harvesting water for irrigation purposes. But most of the tribes of Purulia, except may be only Santhals, lack such indigenous techniques because traditionally they were not well versed with the art of cultivation which was the prime reason for inward migration during pre-colonial and colonial times.

However, after the loss of the forest cover and in desperation, the tribals switched to agriculture but needed constant support in their endeavour. Bandh is a kind of pond that deposits the running down rain water that can be used for irrigation. In terms of policy the government cannot be faulted as the need of Bandhs in the tribal lands was identified as a major communitarian measure to make a dent into the chronic condition of poverty of the tribals. It must be mentioned here that the discussion of tribals in the context of tribals excludes the Santhal tribes. The Santhals being early to agriculture have created their agricultural lands close to water sources and thus are in not that need of bandhs. The second clarification that needs to be made here is that the tribals of various communities stay in clusters but hardly one finds one tribal community shares close proximity with another community. But unfortunately the implementation of the programme throws more questions than answers.

During the field survey the villagers opined that the bandhs are of no use to them in terms of cultivation. They mention the following reasons for such observation.

- *Wrong place*: The villagers are of the view that the places the dams are constructed are no the correct places to store water running down from the hills during rainy season. Their traditional knowledge in following the flow of water was not utilised in selecting the proper place for construction of bandhs. Among the probable reasons for such gross error are many. Creating the bandh at the right place often required digging out stones which is time consuming and expensive. The administration has always been careful about the time factor whereas the contractor has been worried about the expenses. Given the differences that were found to have been sanctioned for the construction bandhs at various places, one gets the feeling the topography of different areas were taken into account while estimating the cost. But in reality, the tribals are of the opinion that corruption was the main factor that prevented the authorities from implementing the programme properly. The district judge has made fine revelations regarding possible corruption in the process. In his report the judge mentions to have been reported by the tribals that put of ₹ 50,000 sanctioned only ₹ 10,000 has been used in construction. In another case the judge verified that the constructed bandh is not in a position to support irrigation.[28]

- *Constructed for Political Purposes not for Agriculture*: As mentioned in the earlier discussion, the tribal communities have been politicised in terms of their numerous presence in a particular area, the bandhs, the tribals feel are created to satisfy political needs of the party in power than actual necessity of the tribals who actually need it. Evidence to this effect is again found on the report of the judge. At Kashidih (also covered during my field survey) the judge reports that a bandh was sanctioned for the Sabars but was actually excavated in the land of some Amulya Singh Sardar. Again at Fuljhore a bandh sanctioned for the Sabars was built in the land of a Santhal. These purposive acts of fraud, the tribals feel is due to political reasons. Those who are in position of influence manage to change the location of the bandhs thus help the programme fail in its objective.

Other Developmental Schemes

Loans

It certainly goes to the credit of the national and state government that they have realised the need for financial support to the tribals to make them self sufficient. There is no dearth of schemes to provide income generating options. Loan under various heads is the primary. Loans are provided to the tribals through government institutions and the programmes are to be supervised by the local government. Apart from general income generating schemes for the poor, there exist some special schemes for the tribals as well. However, the purpose of this particular study it was not important to look at the number of projects officially sanctioned by the government and the number of projects identified as success by the. Considering the fact that there has been no change to the situation of the tribals even after 6 decades of intervention by the government, it is an attempt to find out the nuances of programme implementation. If loan, the biggest of all the developmental initiatives of the government is taken as an indicator of the performance of the system in ensuring tribal development, it can be said that the development programmes in this district has been mere eyewashes. What emerged from the field survey and was compared with other similar documents is a story of politics aiming at ensuring non-delivery of developmental measure to the tribal beneficiaries. In the three blocks that were covered under field survey, only five tribals admitted to have received loan under some kind of government scheme. this came as a surprise as it cannot be the case since the government data shows disbursement of loans under various schemes to a number of tribals of the blocks / villages under survey. Later it was clarified by local intellectuals that the tribals are directed by "people with vested interest" not to admit to have received any loan if asked by anyone in their absence. In an attempt to understand the reason behind such a direction and the source of such a direction, it was revealed that there could be two possible reasons for such denial. One if the asking person has some philanthropic motive, he would be tempted to rush in help to the locality and the second explanation, and the more interesting one, was it might bring the open of cans of corruption involved in the entire process of disbursement of loan. Some case of corruption were reported in a very veiled form and was not clarified to the level of recording but it was understandable that the tribals are afraid of divulging information of loan. But the district judge who had conducted a thorough review of the programmes in the district in his official capacity has recorded cases of tribal deprivation in every detail. Though his report (annexure to this study) makes some mention about the anomalies, his tour diary is a record of gross misappropriation of developmental fund earmarked for poor tribals.

In a village called Mairadih, a tribal informed the judge that some Atul Mahato has taken 50 per cent of loan sanctioned to him. In another place a tribal complained that ₹ 1200 was sanctioned against his name but he got only ₹ 200 and the rest were taken away by some

Ardhendu Pal.[29] The judges Tour diary and final report is filled with evidence of fraud in allocation of loans to the tribals and its misappropriation.

Instead of going on verifying all the anomalies mentioned in the report of the judge it was desired to obtain information about the approach of the authorities towards the plight of the tribals and the way they implement the development programmes. In this context a visit to the West Bengal Scheduled Caste and Scheduled Tribes Development and Finance Corporation was an eye opener. It had a deserted look at 12 noon. Only one person was available and who agreed to talk under the condition of anonymity. Some of his observations were enough to make out why the developmental programmes are not properly implemented. Below is a case to case basis analysis of the problems the authorities put forward.

Insufficiency of the Project

The implementing authorities complain that the targets set by the government are not sufficient for the area to be covered. They are of the view that given the community lifestyle of the tribals, it is not possible to implement a programme with some of the population leaving others. It is a valid argument by the authorities but in the context of the under developed tribals of the district it can be said that they stay in hamlets not consisting more than 10 families the argument that half implementation would create social tension does not hold valid.

Insufficient Manpower

A very valid argument as it was seen that the officc was deserted. The reasons for lack of manpower was the lack of basic facilities at the grass roots level where government 'babus' don't want to remain posted for long. But it can be said that the argument of lack of manpower is more relational than real. The well established fact that bureaucracy is over recruited is the causing a sense of lack of manpower. The real point is lack of willingness to work for the development of the tribals in an uncomfortable environment.

Lack of Supervision

Most of the recent developmental programmes are planned to be undertaken in coordination the local self-government, who are to supervise over the implementation and at this level there seems to be want of attitude. A very valid observation, which was also expressed by the villagers as well. The possible reason for such political aloofness is due to the misplaced priorities. The political establishment is worried about only that section of the population who need facilities, may they not be needing them the most, in order to pledge allegiance to the party. This means only those groups that are aware and organised enough to assert their rights with the political and administrative establishment get the attention of the political class only out of fear of losing the number of their votes. Marginal tribal communities do not figure in their scheme of things thus they do not bother to take interest in the developmental initiatives meant for the tribals.

Non-repayment of Loan by the Tribals

The authorities (the respondent) had interesting explanation to this phenomenon. In his own words the recovery of loans under various schemes meant for the tribal poor was excellent up to a point. But slowly the rate of recovery fell. The reason is the government did not encourage those who repaid the loan in time rather *helped those who defaulted* thus those who wished to repay chose not to repay any further. The second explanation was interesting and explains the politics that ensures tribal underdevelopment. In his words, "it is found that persons other than the targeted person is getting the benefit of the programme." To put it in the form of an example,

> A tractor is bought to a tribal as loan. The objective is to provide him a durable asset for his gainful employment. It is found that after some time the neighbour of the tribal is getting richer. The tribal remains where he was. The process of transfer of gain is very simple. The tribal being low on awareness does not know how to manage the business of tractor and others belonging to advanced economic background ensure that he does not get sufficient business. In the event two things happen. Either the tribal is forced to transfer the ownership to a non-tribal who can run the business in return of some money or the tribal remains as the driver of his own tractor where as the all the business is conducted by the non-tribal neighbour who keeps all the profit.

The natural fallout o such an arrangement is that the tribal will never be in a position to own the tractor and earn a permanent gainful employment though the loan gets repaid in time in the interest of the non-tribal enjoying profit from the use of the tractor.

The actual reasons for non-repayment of the loan amount are basically three. Continuous support in the form of operational knowledge is not provided to the tribals making it difficult for them to initiate and sustain a gainful employment. Second, the tribals, owing to their subsistence livelihoods status use the money meant for initiating a new means of livelihood, end of spending the money in consumption. Third and the only reason that lead to other two reasons is misappropriation of a large portion of the loan amount by middlemen. This makes the amount obtained by the tribal insufficient for initiating a new livelihood option and spending the meagre amount on consumption. One fourth explanation is that the tribals remain indebted throughout the year and thus end of borrowing money from the nearby mahajan who is more often than not a non-tribal. And whenever a tribal gets a loan, a major portion is taken away by the mahajan on the pretext of repayment of his loan.

Other Programmes and Problems

National Rural Employment Guarantee Scheme (NREGS)

The thought behind this national policy is to provide 'food' for a period of time when a particular section of the society are likely to remain without food. The reason for remaining without food is obviously lack of employment opportunity. Keeping aside the national shame that is covertly accepted while conceptualising such a scheme, it must be said about the sensitivity of the national government to think about providing job opportunity and means of earning food for a particular period of time. Let us measure the utility of the scheme in the context of unavailability of job for the tribals of the district. It has been discussed earlier that tribals have two alternatives during the period of agricultural lean. Either loan from non-institutional sources or to migrate out of the area in search of livelihoods options. And the period of migration has been found to be somewhere between three to six months. The government of India has with all wisdom fixed the period of joblessness at an average 100 days in a year. Which, in all practical senses reasonable if there are fair means of livelihoods for the rest of the year. Without going into the practical utility of the scheme or a particular area such as the district of Purulia, one should focus on the implementation o the programme in relation to the objective of the scheme. according to the norms the scheme is applicable to the poor people meaning there by those who fall under the "Below Poverty Line"(BPL). Those who want to avail the opportunity of working under this particular scheme have to prove their credentials of being persons below poverty line. it has been made amply clear that the level of awareness among the tribal leaves no doubt that they understand what BPL means and how to get this particular certificate of shame. However, the government has, as in all other parts of the country, been generous to prepare its own list of persons BPL. In the context of Purulia, it was found that most of those who are actually Below Poverty line are not included in the list. The reason is most of them could not furnish the certificate of domicile and establish their lineage. Most of the tribal communities, being nomads had no one place of residence in the past. During the field survey we came across villages established as recently as last ten years ago. It was reported that peole belonging to BPL category have been left out but and people fairly above the line of poverty have been included in the list. This apart even if the tribals manage to obtain the credible certificate of belonging to the section below poverty line there is no guarantee that the tribals are entitled to avail the opportunity of job and livelihoods option for a certain period of time in the year. The process of availing the job under the scheme is so complicated that those who languish at the bottom of the economic hierarchy primarily because of their lack of awareness would certainly miss out on this opportunity.

Another interesting feature of this scheme is that in the event of a poor fulfilling all the criteria for eligibility to avail the work opportunity under the scheme and the government's inability to prodive job and thus livelihood opportunity, the government remains committed to provide unemployment allowance for the period it failed to provide job from the day of the tribal's first application for job under the scheme, only the waiting period may normally be somewhere between one to two months. In comparison to the objective of the scheme being providing job opportunity for persons BPL and thus ensure livelihoods options for the lean period of the year, a two months is counter productive as people who really need the scheme cannot wait for two years to avail the opportunity. They would rather choose other options such as migration. Now a final word about the accountability of the government in the event of its failure to provide job and unemployment allowance. Provisions are there that a tribal/poor can lodge a complain to get compensation for the period and unemployment. It seems that the government seems to be in no mood to accept accountability on this count. I was provided with a list of unsettled complains lodged in the year 2005. The list consists 78 cases involving more than two thousand tribals. But this is the list of just one year.[30]

Forest Policy and Tribal Development

Before discussing the forest policy of the national and the state government, it is imperative to have a brief discussion on the process of tribal alienation from the forest resources. As discussed earlier in the discussion and in various studies that the tribals were systematically from their forest residency by the Aryans and Aryanised high-caste people.[31] This process, starting in the pre-colonial times, continued throughout the colonial period. It was supposed to stop and attempts were to be taken to restore tribal possession on the forests. The government of India, arguably, started the process of restoring tribals to the forest. In 1956 Government of India nationalised the forest. The ambition of such a policy was to the take possession of the forests from the zamindars who were in possession of a large section of the forest resource of the country. A vast portion of forest of Purulia district was under private ownership. Therefore, the policy of the Government was lauded. But the gap in declaration and implementation of the nationalisation of forest was something that was exploited in such a manner that that, at least for the tribals of Purulia, it proved to be the must important landmark in the process of their alienation from forest. The nationalisation of the forest was declared in 1956 but it was actually implemented in the year 1960. this gap of four years were used by the owners of the forest to engage in large-scale deforestation and turning the forest into large tracts of agricultural land. May be irrelevant, but may be mentioned here that the labour used in this process of deforestation was of the tribals themselves. This could be possible due to the traditional patron-client relationship that existed between the tribal subjects and the non-tribal Mahajan (Zamindar). This alienated the tribals in unprecedented scale.

This was not immediately followed by measures to restore tribal possession over the forests and the exploitation of the forest continued in the name of modernisation of the nation and development. After a long apathy, joint forest management emerged within the context of growing criticism of management priorities and practices of state forestry agencies during the mid 1970s. Protests and resistance on the part of indigenous groups and forest-dependent communities in various regions of the country led environmental scholars and activists to accuse state forestry agencies of bias toward urban and industrial interests to the disadvantage of these groups. In response to these criticisms as well as changing economic conditions in the forestry sector, the Indian government intervened, through parliamentary legislation, to convert forestry from a "state subject" to a "concurrent subject" (i.e., forest policies were to be concurrently developed by state and national governments), and promoted the concept of "social forestry" as the vehicle for increased local participation in forest management.

Since the objective of the study is not to discuss the details of each of the policies of the government and find their relative success and failure, such a discussion is thought not warranted here. Just to pick up one case that has relevance to assumption of the study that there is a politics to ensure the indebtedness of the tribals, the provision of allowing the tribals to cultivate a kind of grass (*Babui Ghass*). The first impact of the policy was further deforestation as all wanted to cultivate the grass at one compact place and cultivate as much as possible. The tribals are also culprits, if their economic condition is ignored, in the eyes of law. But the interesting fact that came to light that non-tribals have obtained lease of vast tract of forest land that are fit for growing the said grass and the tribals are employed as daily wage labourers, engaged in cultivating and cutting the grass, and making the rope and deposit with the lease holder.

The second policy related to the forests and the tribals is the decision of the government to issue pattas against those greenery less forest that are under private possession. Prashant Rakshit, a prominent social worker associated with Paschim Banga Kheria Sabar Kalyan Samiti hailed this policy as a triumph of their cause. But the nuance of the law was well opposed by the innocent minds of the tribals. The law says that those who are in possession of greenery less forest area for a minimum period of five years up to December 2005 are to be issued pattas against those plots of land. The tribals had two simple questions.

1. Does the Government know that tribals are traditionally nomads and hardly settle at a place for that long to clear the

forest (to make it greenery less) and possess the land for five years?

2. Is the Government unaware that tribals do not clear forest for whatever purposes (*aamra bonbashi. Bonbashira bon nasto korena*)? Why does the government think that all the tribals are settled in forest land and have captured forest area?

A third question can be added: did the Government think that the tribals had a five year premonition of such a policy? The tribals' explanation is that the policy is aimed as legitimising the encroachment of forest land by the non-tribals. A Santal respondent argued that whenever the tribals go to the authorities with the request of issuing patta of a land they have possessed for a considerable period of time, the authorities drive them away citing the very arguments cited above. The experience of development initiatives for the poor is nothing short of a disaster in terms of it reaching to the targeted population. For reasons evident by their own explanations, they blame the current political dispensation for their continuous plight even after the reign of sociality ideology in the state for over three decades.

Notes and References

1. Hollis Chenery (1970), Montek Ahluwalia, Clive Bell, John Duloy and Richard Jolly (Oxford: OUP), *Redistribution with Growth.*
2. Walter Fernandes, (1997), "Post-Independence Policies, Planned Development and Tribal Deprivation," in J.S. Bhandari and Subhadra Mitra Channa *Tribes and Government Policies*, (New Delhi: Cosmo Publications), p. 162.
3. R.C. Verma (2003), *Terror by Hunger*, (New Delhi: Aravali Books International Pvt. Ltd.) p. 96.
4. *Ibid.*, pp. 99-100.
5. Timothy Besley and Robin Burgess (2000), "Land Reform, Poverty Reduction, and Growth: Evidence from India," *Quarterly Journal of Economics*, vol. 15, no. 2, May, p. 389. (389-430)
6. CPI(M) Policy Document on Tribal Question (Adopted by the Central Committee in its meeting held on March 2-3, 2002), http://www.cpim.org.
7. CPI(M) Policy Document on Tribal Question (Adopted by the Central Committee in its meeting held on March 2-3, 2002), http://www.cpim.org.

8. The Left Front Government of the state which is in power uninterruptedly since 1977 claims that the successful implementation of land reforms is the principal reason for its continuous rule.
9. Pranab Bardhan and Dilip Mookherjee (2003), *Political Economy of Land Reforms in West Bengal 1978-1998*, June 24.
10. *Ibid*, p. 1.
11. Jean Dreze, Peter Lanjouw and Nareesh Sharma, (1998) "Economic Development 1957-1993," in Peter Lanjouw and Nicholas Stern (Oxford: OUP), *Economic Development in Palanpur over Five Decades.*
12. Pranab Bardhan and Dilip Mookherjee (2003), *Political Economy of Land Reforms in West Bengal 1978-1998*, June 24, p. 12.
13. S.P. Sinha, "Land Tenure, Ownership and Alienation in Bihar, West Bengal and Orissa," in S.N. Mishra (ed.) (1998), *Antiquity to Modernity in Tribal India Vol. III: Ownership and Control of the Resources among Indian Tribes*, (New Delhi: Inter-India Publications) pp. 86-87.
14. *Ibid.*, p. 87.
15. *Ibid.*, p. 94.
16. Budget Statement, Demand No. 36 for the year 2008-09, Land and Land Reforms Department, Government of West Bengal, 2008.
17. Government of West Bengal. The Figures are as on March 15, 2008. Cited in V.K. Ramchandran (2008), "Land Reform Continues in West Bengal," http://www.pragoti.org/node/1875, 22 August. Article courtesy *The Hindu.*
18. Budget Statement, Demand No. 36 for the year 2008-09, Land and Land Reforms Department, Government of West Bengal, 2008.
19. Annexure V to the affidavit submitted to Calcutta High Court in 2002 by the then Chief Secretary to the Government of West Bengal Mr. S.N. Roy.
20. Arup Das, *Op.Cit.*
21. Arup Das, p. Rpt. 11.
22. Arup Das, p. Rpt. 13
23. Applications for restoration of possession by the sons of Sri Sarup Mandi. See Annexure. This case also figured in the local news paper, see annexure
24. Report of the Chief Secretary to the Government of West Bengal, *Op. Cit.*
25. Arup Das, *Op. Cit.*
26. Arup Das, *Op. Cit.*
27. Arup Das, Tour Diary.
28. Arup Das, p. Rpt. 15.
29. Arup Das, p. Tour Diary. 6. For details on allocation, misappropriation

of loan amount sanctioned to tribals, see the final report of the district Judge (annexure).

30. For details, see annexure.
31. E.T. Dalton (1872), *Descriptive Ethnology of Bengal*. Reprinted by the Government of West Bengal, Calcutta, 1972. W.W. Hunter (1883), *Annals of Rural Bengal*. Reprinted in Calcutta, (1965).

V

Economic, Socio-political Conflict within the District

The Contemporary Scenario

Class Nature of the Emerging Society

It is natural that after prolonged and planned exploitation of certain sections of the population by certain other sections and their agents, an unequal society would emerge. The present society of Purulia is divided and arranged in a hierarchical order. More importantly there exist fault lines between various sections of the society. Is such a society, where the economic ordering is neither egalitarian nor meritocratic and the social order is not harmonious, there are bound to be trouble of economic, social and political nature. The present chapter discusses the fault lines, the issues and the conflicts that characterise the present society of Purulia.

Tribal Vs Non-Tribals

The current profile of the tribals reveals an interesting fact in terms of control over the resources. It is to be mentioned here that the condition of all tribal communities is not the same. Among the tribal communities, the most deprived are the Sabars who languish at the bottom of the economic hierarchy of the district. But so far as a comparison with the non-tribals of the district the tribals can be clubbed into one group. The comparison is clear from the discrepancy of livelihoods data for all sections of the population and for the tribals. The tribals lag behind the forward caste population in all parameters of livelihoods. The landholding size of the tribals can be the indication of the wide gap between the tribals and the non-tribals. The Average size of tribal land holding in the three surveyed blocks was found to be = 1 acre. From the government records it can be computed that the actual landholding size of the tribals is certainly below one acre. Whereas, the average landholding size of the non-tribals is somewhere between 4-5 acres per family. The difference in status can get clearer if the asset base of the tribals is compared to that of the non-tribals. The average asset value of a tribal is somewhere around Rupees 5,000 to 10,000.[1] In comparison to this, the asset base of the non-tribals is somewhere around Rupees 1,50,000 to 2,00,000. Such wide gap between two sections of the society has persisted for a very long period of time. It is the ignorance of the tribals and the low level of awareness that has prevented the evolution of the class in itself concept among them. All these while they failed to realise the reason for their chronic poverty. They fail to see that there is a politics behind it that ensures their continuous poverty. It is off late, after their prolonged exposure to the outside world and their interaction with Non-governmental organisations that they have come to be aware of their rights. But it cannot be said for sure that the awareness is enough where the tribals can demand for their rights.

However, the issue of conflict between the tribals versus the Non-tribals was existent form the time they came in each others contact. The non-tribals had the opportunity to feast on the local resources which naturally belonged to the indigenous population and particularly the tribals. A distinction between the indigenous population and the tribals must be further made here to keep the focus of the discussion. Some of the non-tribals have habited the district for long enough to be called indigenous. But for this purpose, tribals are identifies as indigenous as they were at a point in total control of the resources of the district from which they have been slowly alienated by the non-tribals. Initially it was a conflict over resources between the tribals and the non-tribals in which the non-tribals had to win by virtue of their developed mind and exposure to better techniques of livelihood sustenance. But this natural conflict slowly got institutionalised and the non-tribals assumed the positions irreversible superiority. The tribals were permanently pushed to a condition from where it was difficult neigh impossible for them to come out. The nature of conflict then became one sided. The non-tribals kept on exploiting the tribals and the tribals kept on giving in to the exploitative methods of the non-tribals. Forcible eviction of the tribals from their firm and homestead lands became the order of the day. The process is still continuing. According to Dr. Chandidas Mukherjee, author of the Book *Stigmas of Kheria Sabars,* tribals in some parts of the district are still being evicted from their lands. It is specifically true to the tribal communities like Sabars who are in minority and are highly unorganised owing to their low awareness level.[2]

The other one sided conflict that characterised the relationship of the tribals with the non-tribals is atrocity against the tribals. The non-tribals used all means to frighten the tribals. The tribals remain frightened even today. The number of atrocities may have reduced but is not completely over. The victims of such atrocity are primarily those tribal communities that remain unorganised and numerically inferior to others in a comparison. During the study, the villagers and representatives of non-governmental organisations described stories of atrocity that can be termed inhuman at the least. In an unbelievable narration it was revealed some Jagadish Tiwari, a local landlord shot down a tribal like one kills a bird. A tribal was trying to break a twig from his neem tree for brushing teeth. The landlord Mr. Tiwari could see him and without any questioned asked brought out his gun and shot the tribal down. There are also stories about Mr. Tiwari using his muscle power to pick tribal girls for sexual purposes. In another case, a Sabar was publicly lynched by upper caste people (mainly Mahatos). The case that was framed against Hari Sabar was of stealing rice from the shop of a local Mahato. The case was not referred to the police rather the forward caste people took law into their own hands and killed the Sabar in full public view. In another case a Sabar was hit by a forward caste person. The police refused to register a case against the forward caste person who committed the crime. In another case two Mahato boys raped a Sabar girl called Arati Sabar. Police arrested the two culprits but let them go free.[3] A tribal boy (Sabar) made a personal revelation that he was picked up by the police on charges of rape and murder of a classmate. It took ten year for him to be proved to be innocent by the court. The tribal boy is of the view that he was charged for two purposes. One it would be easy for the Mahato boy to escape punishment as the stigma against the Sabars to be born criminals is still persisting and the police would easily believe that the Sabar boy has committed it. The second reason, the boy feels is the anger of the forward caste that this boy was the only boy who was studying and studying well and could have been a challenge to their authority in the future. That is why the planned to ruin his career by implicating him in a case. He emphasised the point that he was picked up on the day of his M*adhyamik* (10th) examination. The atrocities against the tribals is in no way limited to these few examples.

At present, due to increasing interaction with the outside world, the tribals are gaining awareness and realising that the aliens or the non-tribal population of the locality are primarily responsible for their pauperised condition that has become their identity. It was reported that the non-tribal population of the locality treat the tribals as sub-humans and tease them with their caste and profession. It was revealed that the forward caste people do not allow the tribals to share seats in the schools or at other public places. Tribal boys and girls are advised to go and join their parents in generating income for the family rather then wasting time treading at schools as schools and education are not a tribal's cup of tea.

Tribal Vs Tribals

Traditionally, tribals were never an organised unit and that probably explains their lack of share in the national resources. This district is no exception to this. The tribals remain divided. In the past there had been class conflict between various factions among the tribals of the district. The conflicts were primarily related to land, forest resources and occasional crime committed by the member of one particular community against another community. Of late this class conflict has intensified and the primary factor responsible for such intensification is the depleting resource of the locality. The forest that used to be the common property of the tribals is no longer their own. The forest being vast provided the cushion to contain intermittent conflict but in the absence of this vast resource the struggle has come to centre around access to land. It is natural that in every place there cannot be perfect balance in terms of presence of population belonging to all the communities. As we know there are 11 tribal communities inhabiting the district and most of them, other than Santals, were nomads thus kept changing their residence. This has resulted in an uneven distribution of various tribal communities throughout the district. It was notices that in all places, the numerically superior tribal community asserts more control over the resources in that area. Conflicts over land between Sabars and Mundas, Sabars and Oraon, Mundas and Santals are common.

Among the tribals the Santals are the most conscious and organised community among the tribals. They are a deprived section in the district but in comparison to other tribal groupings they are better placed. It is noticed that next to the forward caste population, the Santals occupy the second rank in terms of economic achievement. In a sense it is time for them to make the history repeat for themselves. As it is known that the entire Jungle Mahal area was dominated by the Santals and it were they who had laboriously cleaned the forest and readied the land for cultivation. But due to the process of inward migration and the subsequent systematic exploitation of the tribals in the hands of the non-tribals, they lost their control over land and other natural resources. But one thing was for certain true at leas to this district that the Santals were the first to come in contact with the non-tribals and had got sanskritised much before the other tribal groups got an exposure to the outside world. It was through this process of sanskritisation that they learnt the art of livelihood at the expenses of others.

A phenomenon that was conspicuous in the district was the relative advancement of the Santal tribal community vis-à-vis other tribal communities. At a place called Aam Jharana,[4] the Santals were found to be living close to the Sabars. But there was a distinct difference between the economic condition of the two communities. The Santals were found to be having larger landholdings in comparison to the Sabars. While the Sabars were seen to be lacking proper housing and clothing, the nearby Santals were found to be flaunting their relative affluence. This needed a deep probe as this threatened my basic premise that the tribals are victims of "politics of indebtedness." Unfortunately, the findings supported my hypothesis.

The Santals were not as well off even 20 years earlier as they look to be today. The natural question that came to mind that the Santals were the first victims of exploitation in the hands of the non-tribals as they were to be disposed from their right to land if the non-tribals wanted to establish their control over the resources of the locality. Then how come they are in better place than other tribals communities who came within the ambit exploitative network of the non-tribals? The answer was not easy because the question was accurate. After persistence inquiry and research with an open mind, the reason could be deciphered.

It is true that the Santals were the first to face the aliens or the inward migrants to the district but their exploitation was complete in very short span of time. The only thing they had to lose was their control over land. Permanent settlement and its subsequent abolition ensured the end of the Santali system of management of land. The land then was transferred to the hands of the non-tribals through the method of non-institutional credit pattern that was (in some cases still prevalent) in operation in the olden days. The pattern was simple. Increase the expenditure of the tribals (in this case the Santals) and they would be vulnerable to the process (politics) of indebtedness. The Santals lost their hard earned lands to the non-tribals in very short span of time. By that time other communities were owning land as and when the forest was depleting.[5] Thus, after the loss of Santal lands, they became redundant for the non-tribals as there were emerging classes of people with land.[6] Thus the focus of exploitation shifted to other communities and the Santals were left relatively unaffected by the process of exploitation.

There came a big change in the life of state and thus for the district. A socialist government came to power promising to establish an egalitarian society wherein the resources of the locality would be 'equitably' distributed. According to Mr. Sadhu Singh Sardar, a prominent social activist involved in tribal issues, the tribals had supported the Left Front Government for their promise of land and better access to livelihood resources. But after a rule of more than three decades the tribal poor are in a state disillusion and do not go where to go. In a group discussion a Santal respondent and a Mahato respondent were of the opinion that the ruling party has successfully established an agent class among the tribals. The community from which the agents are to be drawn were decided on the numerical strength of the commuities present at each place. But both of them were of the same opinion that most often than not the agents are drawn from the Santal community the relatively developed community among the tribals. Fault lines have been politically created between the Santals and other tribal communities. The programme of Land Reforms has been used to the best effect in ensuring tension between Santals and other communities of the district. Some of the tribals belonging to communities complained that the lands that have been allotted to them are under the possession of the Santals and the Santals enjoy political patronage. The moment these tribals try to obtain possession, there is risk of inter-community conflict. Cases were reported where such violence has taken places. Tribals belonging to other communities also were of the opinion that under the patronage of the ruling party are discretely exploiting the tribals. During the field survey, it was discovered that the Santals are running illegal country liquor shop close to the habitation of other tribal communities and inducing the other tribals to the habit of drinking there by increase their indebtedness.

Political Class Vs Non-Political Class

The role of the political class in the district is viewed by most of the respondents as most important in the evolution of the present unequal class system that has become characteristic feature of the society in the district. Describing the role of the political class in the district, a journalist who has worked among the tribals for more than 30 years, said the present situation of the tribal has not changed from what it was 50 years ago and also expressed his pessimism that the tribal situation is not going to change in coming 25 years. He feels that during this long stint of the present Left Front government what it has managed to do is that it has created some agents in every village (*gato tirish bochore Baam Front Sarakar somoye jeta hoyechhe, seta holo pratyekti grame kichhuta 'Khore' toiri hoyechhe*). The responsibility of these agents is to ensure vote for the ruling party during the time of election and the ruling party would support the agent in whatever way he increase his wealth. This according to many is the primary bane of the district and the tribals. Another respondent expressed the view that the present ruling party was with the people for the initial 10 years of coming to power but after that has left thinking about the general public. It is only interested in votes and money. Naming particular leaders, tribal respondents questioned the merit of the children of such leader who are the only capable persons of the district to represent and/or be appointed to all government posts of the district. Reacting to the question of possible inaction on the part of the bureaucracy that can be responsible for non-implementation of the developmental programmes in the district, a tribal respondent (also a social activist) Mr. Sadhu Singh Sardar opined that it is true that there is administrative apathy in the district but the root cause, is the apathy of the political party in power as it is the duty of the representatives to articulate the problems of the tribals and make the bureaucracy work towards removal of these problems.

The current situation of the district can be described as a society divided on pclitical lines. If you belong to the political class you enjoy control over the local resources, it you pledge unconditional support to the ruling dispensation, you are allowed to live at least a subsistence life and if you dare protest, you are eliminated or punished heavily.

Economic, Socio-political Conflict within the District

In the contemporary scenario, there is tension between the indigenous population and inward migrants all over the country. Not necessarily the tensions are always violent, but an innate apathy can be easily observed in the behaviour of these two sections of the populations of any locality. Inward migration to the tribal areas all over the country has caused displacement, deprivation and alienation of the indigenous community from the local physical resources. Purulia is a glaring example of indigenous community being exploited by the inward migrants. This had to create socio-political tension in the district and it is quite visible in parts of the district. The most extreme form of manifestation of this conflict is the emergence of People's War Groups or the Naxals or the "Maoists". During my field investigation I came across many who were picked u by the police in charges of being involved in "anti-national" activities. In other wards these are the people who are branded as Maoists of sympathisers of Maoists. It could not be ascertained if there are actually Maoists in the district. This conclusion was arrived at afer realising that those who are alleged to be spreading havoc in the district and are called as Maoists did not seem to have any understanding of the ideals of Mao or Maoist revolution. According to a correspondent of a prominent Bengali daily, the so called Maoist movement in the state and in the district are not organised activity of any kind.

The detailed discussions on various aspects of the lives of the tribals and the failure of the government in addressing the problems have left the tribals in appalling condition. History is filled with testimonies that people raise in revolt against the state when they expect nothing more than only trouble from the state. The condition of the tribals of Purulia district gave the impression that the people have lost al hopes about any favour from the government they had put great hopes on. In this context it is important to recapitulate the rise and fall of the Naxal Movement of the 1960s and recent resurgence of protest called 'Maoism' in the state of West Bengal. In 1967 West Bengal experienced the rise of protest movement called the Naxal movement owing its name to Naxalbari village in the Darjeeling district. The main idea behind the movement was a prolonged struggle against the class enemy identified as the vicious state machinery. The movement had spread to other parts of West Bengal and also to Orissa and Andhra Pradesh. The movement was marred by both heroic and lumpen acts by thousands of guerrillas.

The aim of the Naxal movement was to promote and build a "revolutionary opposition" in order to establish "revolutionary rule" in India. Charu Mazumdar, the ideologue of the Naxal movement advocated that the peasants and lower classes must overthrow the government and upper classes that pursue a capitalistic culture in India by putting the proletariat in a state of plight.

Under the leadership of Charu Mazumdar, the objective set by the naxalite cadres was 'seizure of power through an agrarian revolution'. Their motto was to replace the old feudal order with one that would implement land reforms and free the poor from the clutches of landlords. The tactics adopted to achieve their objective was guerilla warfare. The movement was planned as, almost, a replica of the communist movement under the leadership of Mao Zedong in China. They visualized 'liberation' of territories and they thus hoped to set up 'liberated zones' gradually in different parts of the country that would eventually merge into a territorial unit under Naxalite hegemony.

When Indian communist movement was already there, what was the need for another radical left movement? It was the ineffectiveness of the communist movement and the callous attitude of the then communist leaders in highlighting and fighting for the issues and problems of the downtrodden classes like peasantry, dalits and tribal communities that insisted the young radicals in the left parties break out of the Marxist fold and form their own group on Maoist line of Revolutionary Communism.

Born in a small village of West Bengal, the Naxalite ideology gained popularity among youth and intellectual circle in many parts of India within a few years. The Naxalites organized the All India Coordination Committee of Communist Revolutionaries (AICCCR) and peasants' uprisings were organized in several parts of the country. On April 22, 1969 the Communist Party of India (Marxist-Leninist) was formed by AICCCR to give the radical factions believing in the Naxal ideology a political platform to highlight various issues for political mobilisation. By the early 1970s, Naxalite movement had its presence in many states like Andhra Pradesh, Orissa, Bihar, Uttar Pradesh etc. For some time the naxalite guerillas had virtually set up alternate administrative machinery in Srikakulam of Andhra Pradesh, to which they referred to as 'liberated zone'. In parts of Bihar and Uttar Pradesh, the Naxalites succeeded in mobilizing the peasantry to recover lands they had lost to the moneylender-cum-landlords whom they had mortgaged their properties in lieu of money. In Punjab rich landlords and policemen were targeted by bands of Naxalites. In Midnapur and Birbhum of West Bengal armed peasants' struggle broke out. In Andhra Pradesh, Orissa and West Bengal, the Naxalites found their main support among the peasantry and the aboriginal tribal communities, who had been the most oppressed and marginalized segment of Indian society.

The popularity of naxalbari movement and growing strength of Naxal groups alarmed the government of India to set up a committee for looking into the matter. The committee, in its report revealed that the basic cause of unrest was the defective implementation of laws enacted to protect the interests of the poor farmers and tribals. But, instead of taking measures to safeguard the rights of farmers and tribals and make them believe the democratic system of governance, government, worried over the law and order situation in the areas of naxal influence, took reactionary steps by raising strong police action against the Naxalites. Through this, the government succeeded in weakening the Naxalite rebellion to some extent. Charu Mazumdar was captured from a Calcutta hideout in July 1972 who died in police custody 12 days after his arrest. This incident raised suspicion about the treatment meted out to him by the police in the custody and the allegation of the ill-treatment meted to the detainees was made by intellectuals across the country, left wing politicians and scholars. However, these developments had a great role in carrying the naxal message to people at the grassroot level of Indian society.

The next hammer on naxal movement and its cadres was the emergency imposed in 1975. Most of the elite members as well as grassroot level leaders of the movement were either put in jails; many veterans went underground to escape arrest. For some time, it seemed, naxal movement would die in India. But it entered a new phase with the end of Emergency and a new government came into power at the center after 1977 general elections. The new and first non-congress government released naxal leaders from jails following a nationwide movement organized by various human rights groups in the country and abroad.

However, the series of developments linked to the naxal movement caused fragmentation in the ranks of naxalism. But almost all the groups committed to the ideology of the movement traced their origin to the common political forum CPI (ML) which was not directly involved in armed rebellion but in propagating the ideology of naxalwari movement and mobilising people in favour of it. On the other hand, the People's War Group (PWG) in Andhra Pradesh and Maoist Communist Centre (MCC) in Bihar preferred to go on the path of guerilla warfare. During the last two decades since the 1980s, these two different streams of the Naxalite movement have been staging armed resistance and rebellion in their respective zones against police force, administration, landlords and business communities.

Dalits, Adivasis and Naxalites

Although the terms of reference did not specifically mention Naxalites (or Maoists), the group's brief was to identify causes of unrest and discontent in areas affected by "widespread displacement, forest issues, insecure tenancies and others forms of exploitation like usury, land alienation and imperfect market conditions…". Clearly, such areas fall in the above-mentioned five states – and significantly enough, the group organised field visits in these areas to observe the situation at first hand, on the basis of which it has come out with stark revelations that expose the culpability of the state in denying the poor their basic rights, the treachery of a corrupt bureaucracy to implement the laws, and its complicity with a trigger-happy police to suppress popular protest.

All these explain, as the report states in unambiguous terms, why the victims of such official crimes support the "extremists" – the term used for Maoists. Maintaining that "the main support for the Naxalite movement comes from dalits and adivasis", the group concentrated on these two sections (termed as scheduled castes and scheduled tribes respectively in official parlance) which comprise about one-fourth of India's population, the majority living in rural areas.

Apart from the high levels of poverty, the dalits suffer from various types of disadvantages like limited employment opportunities, political marginalisation, low education, social discrimination, and human rights violation. As for the adivasi population, besides remaining backward in all aspects of human development including education, health, nutrition, etc, they have been steadily losing their traditional tribal rights and command over resources. The report points out in this connection the administration's failure to implement the protective regulations in scheduled areas, which has resulted in land alienation, forced eviction from land, dependence of the tribals on moneylenders – made worse often by "violence by the state functionaries".

All these facts as described in the report may not come as a surprise to those who have followed the findings of earlier publications like the National Commission on scheduled castes and scheduled tribes; the government of India Report of the Expert Group on Prevention of Alienation of Tribal Land and Its Restoration (2004), as well as the various reports by civil rights groups. But the present report stands out from them in several respects. It explains the causes and success of the Naxalite movement in a particular territorial stretch by locating it in the macroeconomic scene today.

Incidentally, every dalit and adivasi poor in India have not joined the Naxalite movement. There are many states with pockets of high proportion of adivasis and dalits but little Naxalite influence, as in Punjab, Haryana, Gujarat and Rajasthan. The report quite rightly points out that "poverty does create deprivation but other factors like denial of justice, human dignity, cause alienation resulting in the conviction that relief can be had outside the system by breaking the current order asunder". It adds that for such a violent upheaval to happen, there is the likelihood of the "spread of awareness and consciousness". And this is where, as the report suggests, the Maoists have played a significant role by stepping into the craters of dalit and adivasi deprivation in the five states, and organising the deprived for their rights.

Its authors situate the Naxalite movement in the historical context of the "development paradigm pursued since independence", which they assert, has "aggravated the prevailing discontent among marginalised sections of society". While explaining the current surge in Naxalite activities, they slam the neoliberal "directional shift in government policies towards modernisation and mechanisation, export orientation, diversification to produce for the market, withdrawal of various subsidy regimes and exposure to global trade" as "an important factor in hurting the poor in several ways".

Following this conceptual approach, they look at the Maoist movement in a way that is different from the prevalent official attitude which primarily blames the Naxalites for the violence. Instead, the present report lays stress on the "structural violence which is implicit in the social and economic system" and which in the opinion of its authors prompts the radical groups to justify their own violent acts. At the same time, the authors distance themselves from the Naxalites, who "are engaged in a violent fight against the state for overpowering and overthrowing it", and who, they feel "exploit the situation for their own political gain by giving the affected persons some semblance of relief or response. Thereby they tend to legitimise in the eyes of the masses their own legal or even illegal activities." Yet, the authors of the report have to admit that the Naxalites have indeed carried out certain socio-economic reforms in their areas of control.

Purulia

The economic condition of the tribals in this district of West Bengal is against the hopes of the tribals from the state under the rule of Left Front for more than 30 years. The tribals have nothing to look forward to and the state administration is oblivious to their plight. On top of it the political party they had hoped to effect changes in their lives has virtually betrayed their trust and joined hands with those who were and are exploiting the tribals in various ways. Thus, the condition is ripe for any kind of movement that can be initiated by mobilizing the tribals. The current resurgence of violence in the district is certainly an expression of anguish by the tribals. But one thing that comes as a surprise that the tribals who are not enough aware to demand their share from the government developmental resources have all on a sudden become so aware and organized that they would launch a protest movement against the state. This unlikely response of the tribals warranted detailed inquiry of the so called Maoist movement in the district. The real objective of the movement or pure violence in the district could not be checked with the Maoists as it was not possible to contact them. One of the reasons for not getting access to them is that they do not maintain any separate identity. It was reported that any one to every one in the three blocks under study could be a Maoist. This blurring line between the general population and the Maoists can be interpreted as tacit support the so called Maoists enjoy as a force from the locals.

The Approach and the Method

The approach of those who are resorting to violence and are called Maoists by the state political and administrative structure does not match in anyway to the approach of Mao and even that of the earlier Naxal movement of the state. In a group discussion two Tribals and three non-tribals were all of the same opinion that the tribals have no other options but to rise in revolt. The administration and the political structure are all involved in exploitation of the tribals. But the only problem is the lack of awareness among the tribals who do not think about the future. But the tribals have at least realized that the state has to be forced to act. But the tribals feel helpless that they themselves cannot raise the fight against the state and administration. The tribal members of the group were forthright to say that the current situation of the tribals is directly related to the failure of the CPI (M) as a political force to uphold the rights of the tribals.

The tribals look at the so called Maoists as a force that can stand up against the government and force the government to work for the people in general. The so called Maoist upsurge in the district is identified as an explosion of frustration. But it was clear that the tribals do not support the methodology of the so called Maoist forces. The tribals are of the opinion that it would have been better if the so called Maoists adopted non-violent methods instead of violent means. To the obvious next question that followed, are the tribals threatened by the Maoists?, the answer was a unanimous no. Therefore, it can be concluded that the tribals are not violent and do not wish that there should be violence conducted by any agency in the locality may that be the government or the so called Maoists the tribals call '*Bon Party*'. The Bon Party do not disturb the villagers is evident from the fact that the villagers informed that they came across the Bon Party occasionally when they go into the jungle in search o dry twigs but have never been harassed by the Bon Party. Thus, the tribals have no particular reason to be not liking the Bon Party or their methods. But the problem the tribals face due to the presence and activity of the Bon Party comes from the government or the administration, particularly the police. It must be made clear here that the Bon Party adopt a targeted approach in their operation. Their target is limited to the political leadership of the CPI (M) and the police administration. This is the only thing that can be traced to the method advocated by Karl Marx for his class war. But this simile requires the assumption that the present day leadership have assumed the characteristic of the capitalists against whom the class war was advocated by Marx. If the political leadership is to be fought then the first target has to be the state power as the state power provides protection to the political class as in Marx's analysis the state power was used to give protection to the capitalists. In such case, like Karl Marx, the Bon Party feel elimination of the state power (police) is important to reach to the political class who are the prime target of the Bon Party or the Maoists of the district.

The targets of the Maoists are primarily the members of a particular political party, i.e. the CPI (M). Among the prominent leaders killed is Mr. Ravi Kar. Mr. Kar was the district president of CPI (M) in Purulia. He was killed gruesomely. He was burnt to death along with his wife in his own house. During the field investigation attempt was made to understand the reason for killing this particular leader. The villagers of Mr. Kar's locality were of the opinion that Mr. Kar was the target of the Maoists for long for his actions. Among his actions included sponsoring murder of people who refused to follow him. Apart from this Mr. Kar, in the opinion of the locals, was involved in exploiting the tribals through various means and thus had earned the anger of the Maoists. One tribal youth was of the opinion that Mr. Kar got a repayment of his deeds in his own coins. He cited cases suggesting that Mr. Kar was a virtual king in the locality and used to rule on his own whims without paying any respect to the law of the land. The youth even accused Mr. Kar of offending tribal ladies in front of large gatherings. The local people do not seem to have much sympathy for the leaders being killed by the Maoists.

The locals also feel that the current trend of so called Maoist movement is getting closer to just criminal activity. This has two implications. One the Bon Party have lost their ideological ground and have turned into criminal activity in the locality. If this had been the case, the Bon Party would have killed and looted indiscriminately in the district without distinguishing between politically influential and non-political persons. The targeted attack of persons of high political leanings shows the anger towards that particular class. The second implication is that some one else is committing the mindless violence or violence for ulterior motives and he blame is put on the Bon Party. Such a method adopted to settle political scores is a convenient way as the purpose would be achieved with minimal risk. On investigation it came to the fore that there is a distinction between killings of the Maoists[7] and the killings of other kinds which the government calls the acts of Moist violence but the Maoists deny their involvement. In cases committed by the Maoists, there is kind of prior warning about the elimination of certain individual but in other cases thee is no such warning. And the more important factor is the Maoists do not mind owning up their crime since it is done with a purpose which is served by owning up the crime. Thus, the killings the Maoists do not own up has to be believed to have not been committed by them. Now the question is who commits these crimes and the blame conveniently goes to the Maoists or what the tribals call Bon Party.

During field investigation, this question was subtly asked to villagers both tribal and non-tribal. Explanations were also sought from the intellectuals of the locality who are in know of the situation. What emerged is complex and interesting. The villagers are of the opinion that all the crimes committed and not owned up by the Maoists cannot have been committed by the Bon Party as the tribals believe that the Bon Party are too forthright is claiming responsibility for their acts. They feel these crimes are committed by political forces and the responsibility is passed on to the Bon Party as they have an expressed intension of killing political leadership. Then to the question of why the villagers do not believe that the Maoists could have committed the crimes they do not own up, the villagers come up with a prompt answer that "he was not the target".[8] This answer was endorsed and explained by a journalist working for a leading Bengali daily in the locality. According to him the Maoist 'menace' is being used by the political system[9] to eliminate the internally rebellious forces. He gave the following example.

After the killing of Ravi Kar, there was no one to uphold the flag of CPI (M) in Bandwan district and Mr. Ganapati Bhadra was not that prominent a leader that Maoists would target and kill. The killing of Ganapati Bhadra is purely political and may be in combination with illegal business connection. He said there were reports that Mr. Bhadra was involved in illegal mining and export of stones from the locality and had developed enmity with other forces in the same business. Those who wanted to settle scores with him used the opportunity to eliminate him. He was prompt to add that the forces used to commit the crime certainly have linkages with the Bon Party.

On further probe, an interesting complex evolved related to the Maoist activities in the district, the response of the state administration, and its impact. It has turned into a vicious circle. In the opinion of the general public, the economic condition of the district is highly uneven and at the bottom of the economic hierarchy lie the tribals who were marginalized earlier and the had hoped for better fortunes from the Left Front Government that promised a lot of things for the poor, particularly the Scheduled Castes and the Scheduled Tribes. But after the rule of the left front for over three decades the results are for all to see that there has been no dent to the conditions of the tribals at least in this particular district of the state. The condition, thus, got matured for the general population to feel alienated from: the society (as the stigma of belonging to the lower section of the society); from the political system (as in themselves no particular tribal community belonged to the majority coalition to attract the attention of the political structure); from the economic structure (as there remained no scope or earning livelihoods).[10] Now there was a reprisal against the state apathy or state sponsored exploitation. Among many possible ways, violence is one of the ways the frustration got manifested in the district. The state reacted promptly and in its attempt to contain the problem, termed it as a Maoist movement. The police administration in any part of the country has a very effective method of dealing with problems of any kind. It is very easy to term a particular problem as a problem of law and order and obtain the liberty of encroaching upon the civil rights of the general population. Thanks to the administration for not resorting to methods like Salwa Judom but the measures taken by the police in the district are no less effective in producing counter productive sentiments among the tribals. People have been picked up by the police in charges of helping the Maoists. Once some one is picked and identified as a Maoist, he suffers from the stigma and no one offers him any job or shelter out of fear of being harassed by the police. Thus, the person concerned remains vulnerable to inducements to commit criminal activities. Such elements are mostly used by the political forces to commit crimes to eliminate rivals in the name of Maoist Killings.

The intellectuals of the locality are of the opinion that the uprising against the political party in power has no connection what so ever with Maoist movement in other parts of the country. The argument to support this conviction is derived from the fact that the so called Maoists had recently (early November 2008) attacked the Chief Minister's convoy with landmines. The police reacted and in the process committed crimes against the tribals. One particular act of the police angered the tribals the most. A tribal girl was raped and murdered alleged by the police. The tribals responded by cutting the supply to the police force stationed in the locality. It was a spontaneous act in response to police misbehaviour and was supported by the Maoists who called for prolonged *bandhs* in the locality but this, though occurred in the nearby district and had Maoist involvement, did not have any effect in Purulia. There was no protests or *bandhs* in Purulia. This proves the argument that the local uprising cannot be totally called Maoist operation as there seems to have no connection of the forces rising against the administration in the district with Maoists operating in other parts of the state and country.

During interactions with the tribals it was reported by the villagers that there exist Maoist organisation in the dense forests of Purulia and the villagers are convinced that police cannot succeed in eliminating these camps as the terrain is rugged and has a thick forest cover. But what the police ends up doing, according to the villagers, harassing the poor villagers in the name of tackling Maoist menace. Given the subsistence agriculture the tribals are engaged in, they need to supplement their income from agriculture with additional income generated by using forest produce. The use of the forest by the tribals is limited to collection of *Tendu* leafs, *Saal* leafs and dry twigs. For this the tribals need to go to the forest regularly. But the police in the name of dealing with the Maoists, arrests any one it finds coming out of the forest in the evening and harasses the tribals on the pretext of they being either informers for the Maoists of suppliers of food and other essentials. Such act of the police has two effects. It alienates the police force from the local community with whom the police is supposed to work and provide protection. Secondly, it increases sympathy for the forces that dare to stand up against the police.

Local perceptions about the Ideology of the Bon Party

It was important to understand the perception of the local perception towards the so called Maoist forces or the Bon Party. Throughout interactions with the locals it was revealed that the tribals have been contacted by the Maoists for recruitment purposes. Villagers were cautious enough not reveal more information about the pattern of recruitment of the Maoists but revealed certainly that they have never been coerced to send their family members to join their ranks. The villagers who seemed to have followed the Maoist activities in the district were asked to give their opinion on the method and objective of the Maoists. The villagers were clear in their minds that the Bon Party posed no threat to the local population but their presence and activity in the district has brought trouble for the local people from the police. The locals also seemed to be certain that the Bon Party targets only the members of the CPI (M). They further clarified that not all members of CPI (M) are targets of the Bon Party. It is only those leaders who are high in rank or are found to be involved in exploitation of the tribals are the genuine targets of the Bon Party.

On the question of possible objective of the Maoists, the villagers had a simple explanation. They feel it is just a reaction against the ineffectiveness of the political party in ensuring development of the tribal. On the other hand the political party is believed to a part of the exploitative mechanism to keep exploiting the tribals. Thus, the objective of the Maoists, they feel is just to punish those the Bon Party think to be responsible for their condition of perpetual poverty. While the discussion was taken to the level of possible future plans of the Bon Party, the villagers seemed lost.

The question that was sought answer to is "What next after the hypothetical elimination of the present political class?" To this the villagers did not have a convincing answer as they themselves did not have any idea of the future plans of the Bon Party or the Maoists. The villagers were of the view that it is the lack of a future projection that sometimes gives them the feeling that the present movement is not going to be effective in the long run and would eventually fizzle out like any other potential movement lost in history. On the question of leadership to the current so called Maoist movement, the tribal villagers had conflicting answers. Some were of the opinion that the tribals who constitute majority of the strike force are not in the leadership position of the movement. It is the forward caste and forward class people who provide leadership to this movement. The reason for the forward class people doing so, they believe, is a sense of relative deprivation to others in the same class. The second explanation that was put forward was that it is continuation of the Naxal movement of the late 1960s. The leadership is being provided by the remnants of the Naxal movement. This hypothesis is supported by the high level of motivation among the fighting forces and the professionalism in their network and attack. I was taken to a place to witness the nature of attack by the Maoists. It is place called *Dhuarsuni* where the Maoists had blown up a newly constructed tourist lodge. It was a surprise for two reasons. First, the nature of attack gave indication of the attack being carried out by well someone well trained in handling explosives. Secondly, why was an empty tourist lodge attacked?

Some probable explanations were provided by the villagers. It was clear that the place was not that famous as a tourist place. Only a tribal temple existed there and a river flows nearby. Only during the winter some local visit the place for the purpose of picnic. Thus, from all practical point of view, the villagers did not feel the need of

Blown up Tourist Lodge at Dhuarsuni

a tourist lodge at that interior place.[11] There was a guess that the government is constructing this building to transform it into a police post to keep track and tackle the Maoists. "With this guess, the Bon Party caused the blast." This argument goes on to prove the presence of think-tank among the Bon Party and their continuous training and motivation.

The third explanation to the leadership question was provided by the intellectuals of the locality. They provided one of the possibility is that the leadership is provided by the radical faction in the Left Front who are dissatisfied with the performance of the ruling party and are trying to eliminate the corrupt elements from the political establishment. But they even do not rule out the involvement of former naxals and outsiders providing leadership to the movement.

Effects of the movement on the Lives of the Tribals

According to the villagers, the presence of Maoists in the area has brought both trouble and positives. Both comes from the government. In the name of tackling Maoists the police atrocity over the locals has increased. Any one who has ever raised a question against government apathy and corruption is being termed as a Maoist and is being picked by the police and harassed. I came across a person who was termed as Maoist and detained for 12 hours in connection with the murder of Mr. Ravi Kar and his wife. The reason for the administration suspecting him to be a Maoist was his protest against the local contractor paying lesser wage than fixed by the government. His name is Fotik Hamrum, an activist of the Paschim Banga Kharia Sabar Kalyan Samiti. As part of his activity he takes up the cases of the Sabars with the administration, thus got identified as a Maoist. Secondly police enters into the villages of the tribals and ransacks the houses in the name of searching Maoists.

But the tribals seem to be ready to suffer these troubles in comparison to the benefits they think the presence of Maoists have brought to them. It is the perception of the population that the government is not going to act on its own as it has not done so in past. Any amount of pleading by the tribals, they feel falls in deaf years. It is only when the Maoists or the Bon Party started counter attacking the political establishment that the government is now considering developmental initiatives seriously. Though the tribals are not satisfied with present level of activism of the government or the administration but they feel the little shake up that can be marked among the administrative machinery is due to the presence of the Bon Party. The villagers are of the opinion that the Bon Party are getting support from all other legitimate political parties. In other words, other political parties are forced to support the Maoists is in the opinion the local population, the political parties have come to realise that nothing except brute force can bring any change to the system and thus if the Maoists are using that force must be supported. This argument was also supported and endorsed by a local Youth leader Mr. Novendu Mahalik.[12] In the opinion of Mr. Mahalik the current violence is generally condemnable and should not be allowed in a democracy like India. But here the situation is different. As the level of awareness among the tribals is very low, therefore it is impossible to mobilise them for a prolonged political movement. Secondly, during the Left Front rule of over three decades, the Left Front has ensured that the tribals remain marginalised and unaware for generations. Thirdly, the fear psychosis created by the CPI (M) among the tribals prevents the tribals from coming into open confrontation with the ruling political party. Thus, he argues that the only option left is the language of force which the Maoists seem to be speaking and other political parties are forced to extend tacit support to the Maoists. An intellectual of Bandwan was of the opinion that the kind of violence occasionally taking place should take place more frequently and at more places throughout Purulia district. He called the protest violence as an outburst against continuous exploitation.

Conclusions

After a fairly long discussion on the condition tribals of Purulia district the following conclusion can be drawn.

Tribals being the first among the indigenous communities of the district had full control over the resources till 'alien' in the form of non-tribals from the coastal areas and followed by the British came into the area. The relative advantage in terms of knowledge of technology enjoyed by the non-tribals was used to trap the tribals into the net of one way exploitation. With permanent settlement, inward migrants who came in primarily as farmers later turned themselves into traders and linked the local resources to the out side world and thus created a never ending flow of resources. But the tribals were kept out side the process of this resource flow.

Improved communication added speed to the flow of resources leaving the tribals stripped of their primary means of livelihoods. The most precious possession of the tribals, the land was slowly and steadily alienated from them through the use of credit. Introduction of money economy in place of barter was one of the principal factors that caused indebtedness of the tribals.

After independence, came the most severe blow to the tribals through the nationalisation of forest and a gap of four years in implementing the policy. The non-tribals who were owners of major portion of the forest, cleared the forest with the use of tribal labour and turned the former forest into agricultural land belonging to the non-tribals.

Discovery of natural resources in the district should ideally have generated income opportunity for the tribals to supplement their meagre income from the low yield small landholdings. But on the contrary fresh batch of aliens came in with new ideas for facilitating the process of tribals exploitation. The opportunities legally created by the discovery of natural resources were soon outnumbered by illegal opportunists who devised ways of drawing tribals out the protection of law and job security to make them work in illegal exploration of local resources. Making the tribals indebted seemed to be the easiest way as most of the tribals in this or in earlier generation have fallen prey to one one's exploitative mechanism. The ignorance of the tribals was useful in smooth exploitation of the tribals.

Parts of the district that do not have industrial resources, exploitation continued in the age ole method of credit. Being at the fringe of the economic arena, the tribals always maintained a subsistence livelihood status that was often marked by shortage. The local predators grabbed the opportunity and established a system that would perpetuate the underdeveloped condition of the tribals and would keep them at the mercy of the non-tribals. The process still continues.

For trouble free exploitation two things were required in a democratic system. A non-reactive subject who would never raise a question and political patronage. The political predators were more than willing to give that protection and be part of the process for mutual benefits and the passivity of the tribal subjects was ensured by keeping them not only poor but also ignorant.

Showing pro-active accountability, the Left Front Government initiated the socialist programme of Land Reforms that aimed at equitable distribution of land the basic resource of the state. The priority target group were the weaker sections of the society particularly the SCs and the STs. As evidence suggested, the programme has brought no real benefits for the tribals. Rampant corruption at every level of governance ensured diversion of funds earmarked for the development of the tribals. The political class also succeeded in establishing agents at the grass roots levels that ensured their repeated return to power in the return enjoyed patronage to get richer at the peril of the tribals. Fault line among tribals were also created to prevent the tribals from putting up united fight against the non-tribals. The stories of other developmental initiatives are no better. Unsuitable policies, indifferent bureaucracy, greedy political establishment, in combination worked towards ensuring perpetual indebtedness of the tribals.

Gradually the situation matured for any kind of reactive explosion but what lacked is leadership to give the reactive explosion a direction. Supposedly, this leadership is being provided by the remnants of the Naxal movement of the late 1960s. It is also believed that radical forces within the ruling dispensation is providing the leadership. But as any other violent movement this (Maoist) movement has also got weaknesses. Criminal activities having no ideological objective are also being committed by the Maoists or in their names. In the name of tackling the menace of Maoism, the (police) administration has started harassing the tribals and reducing their access to the forest, one of their primary means of livelihoods.

The purpose of any academic research is to find solutions to the problems at hand. But the problems for the tribal population of Purulia are so complex and so manmade that one fails to find the point from where corrective measures should be initiated. Abolition of the political class may be a good starting point, just may be.

Notes and References

1. The asset of the tribals include domestic animals such as cows, goats and fighting roosters along with assets such as radio, bicycles, etc.
2. During an interview on 09/12 /2008, at Manbazar, Purulia.
3. Case No. GR 873 of 1992 under section 354 and 324, Barabazar PS. The case is pending before the court.
4. The village was in news for starvation death and nudity.
5. The reason for forest depletion and its impact on the tribal life would form art of another section of the discussion.
6. At a place like Purulia, given the nature of the climate and soil pattern, land is a very precious commodity.
7. The cases owned up by the Maoists according to their sources.
8. Referring to particular cases that are disputed killings
9. He mentioned the name of a particular political party namely the CPI (M).
10. Land reforms, Forest Policy and the Development initiatives are discussed elsewhere.
11. The place where the tourist lodge was constructed is at the foot of a hill covered with thick forest and the forest is supposed to be used by the Maoists for training and hiding purposes.
12. Novendu Mahalik's interview was not conducted with the intension of interacting with any or a particular political party. He was one of the few tribal youths who had good education and could thus talk at length on problems of tribals of the district. It was durin the interaction that he revealed that he belongs to Bharatiya Janata Party.

Bibliography

Primary Sources

Report on Indebtedness among Rural Labour Household, 50th Round on the N.S.S. 1993-1995, Labour Bureau, Ministry of Labour, India, 1997.

The affidavit submitted to Calcutta High Court in 2002 by the then Chief Secretary to the Government of West Bengal Mr. S.N Roy, 2002.

Budget Statement, Demand No. 36 for the year 2008-09, Land and Land Reforms Department, Government of West Bengal, 2008.

CPI(M) Policy Document on Tribal Question (Adopted by the Central Committee in its meeting held on March 2-3, 2002), http://www.cpim.org.

Report of Sri Arup Das, Hon'ble District Judge, Purulia, 2000.

Books

Athreya, V., G. Djurfeldt, and S. Lindberg, *Barriers Broken: Production Relations and Agrarian Change in Tamil Nadu,* New Delhi: Sage, 1990.

Bardhan, P. (ed.), *Conversations Between Economists and Anthropologists,* Delhi: Oxford University Press, 1990.

Beck, Tony, *The Experience of Poverty: Fighting for Respect and Resources in Village India*, London: Intermediate Technology Publications, 1994.

Ben Rogaly, Barbara Harriss- White and Sugata Bose (eds), Sonar Bangla? Agricultural Growth and Agrarian Change in West Bengal and Bangladesh, New Delhi, Sage, 1999.

Binswanger, H.P. and Rosenzweig, M.R., *Contractual Arrangements, Employment, and Wages in Rural Labour Markets: A Critical Review,* New York: Agricultural Development Council, 1981.

Bliss, C.J. and Stern, N.H., *Palanpur: The Economy of an Indian Village*, Oxford: Oxford University Press, 1982.

Bouman, F., *Small, Short and Unsecured: Informal Rural Finance in India*, Delhi: Oxford University Press, 1989.

Breman, Jan, *Beyond Patronage and Exploitation: Changing Agrarian Relations in South Gujarat*, Delhi: Oxford University Press, 1993.

Breman, Jan, *Footloose Labour: Working in the Indian Informal Economy*, Cambridge: Cambridge University Press, 1996.

Breman, Jan, *Of Peasants, Migrants and Paupers: Rural Labour Circulation and Capitalist Production in West India*, Delhi: Oxford University Press, 1985.

Breman, Jan, *Wage Hunters and Gatherers*, Delhi: Oxford University Press, 1994.

Chakravarty, S. (ed.), *The Balance Between Industry and Agriculture in Economic Development, vol. III*, London: MacMillan, 1989.

Chant, S., *Gender and Migration in Developing Countries*, London: Belhaven Press, 1992.

Chenery, Hollis and Ahluwalia Montek ,Clive Bell, John Duloy and Richard Jolly, *Redistribution with Growth*, Oxford: OUP, 1970.

Dalton, E.T., *Descriptive Ethnology of Bengal*, 1872. Reprinted by the Government of West Bengal, Calcutta, 1972. W.W. Hunter, *Annals of Rural Bengal*, 11883. Reprinted in Calcutta, 1965.

Datt, G., *Bargaining Power, Wages and Employment: An Analysis of Agricultural Labour Markets in India*, New Delhi: Sage, 1996.

Davies, S., *Adaptable Livelihoods: Coping with Food Insecurity in the Malian Sahel*, London: Macmillan Press, 1996.

Deogankar, S.G., *Tribal Exploitation: A Study of Victims of Crime and Bondedness,* New Delhi, Inter-India Publications, 1990.

Dharm, Narian. J.W. Mellor and G.M. Desai (Ed.), *Agricultural Change and Rural Poverty: Variations on a Theme*, Baltimore: Johns Hopkins, 1985.

Easton, David, *The Political System: An Inquiry into the State of Political Science*, (New York: Alfred A. Knopf, 1953, p. 129)

Ghate, Rulha S., *Forest Policy and Tribal Development*, New Delhi: Concept Publishing, 1992.

Harriss-White, B., Guhan, S. and Cassen, R.H. (eds), *Poverty in India: Research and Policy*, Oxford: Oxford University Press, 1992.

Hunter, W.W., *Annals of Rural Bengal*, 11883. Reprinted in Calcutta, 1965.

Jenamani, Surendra, *Poverty and Underdevelopment in Tribal Areas: A Geographical Analysis*, New Delhi: Concept Publishing, 2005.

Lipton, Michael, with Longhurst, Richard, *New Seeds and Poor Peoplel*, London: Unwin Hyman, 1989.

Mishra, Girish, *Agrarian Problems of Permanent Settlement,* New Delhi: People's Publishing House, 1978.

Mukhopadhay, Samir Kumar, *Permanent Settlement to Operation Barga*, New Delhi: Minerva Publications, 1994.

Nelson, J.M. "Sojourners versus New Urbanites: Causes and Consequences of Temporary versus Permanent Cityward Migration in Developing Countries," *Economic Development and Cultural Change*, vol. 24, no. 4, pp. 721–57.

Nimbran, Amrik Singh, *Poverty Land and Violence: An Analytical Study of Naxalism in Bihar*, Patna: Layman's Publications, 1992.

Panda, R.K., *Agricultutal Indebtedness and Institutional Finance*, New Delhi: Ashish Publishing House, 1985.

Ramachandran, V.K., *Wage Labour and Unfreedom in Agriculture*, London: Claredon, 1990.

Ramana Murthy, R.V., "Seasonal Labour Migration in Semi-Arid Areas: A Case Study of Palamuuru Labour," M.Phil. Thesis, Hyderabad: Department of Economics, University of Hyderabad, 1991.

Ramzah, P. and Manohar M, *Tribal Indebtedness*, Bombay: Himalaya Publishing House, 1992.

Rao, G.B., *Household Coping/ Survival Strategies in Drought-prone Regions: A Case Study of Anantapur District, Andhra Pradesh*, India SPWD-Hyderabad Centre, 2001.

Rao, U., *Palamoor Labour: A Study of Migrant Labour in Mahabubnagar District*, Hyderabad: C.D. Deshmukh Impact Centre, Council for Social Development, 1994.

Reddy, G. Prakash, *Politics of Tribal Exploitation: A Study of Tribal Unrest in Adilalbad*, Delhi: Mittal Publications, 1987.

Roychowdhury, Birendra Kishore, *Permanent Settlement and After*, Calcutta: Book Company, 1942.

Sen, Sachin, *Permanent Settlement in Bengal*, Calcutta: M.C. Sorkar and Sons, 1933.

Singh, I.J., *The Great Ascent: The Rural Poor in South Asia*, Baltimore: Johns Hopkins, 1990.

Skeldon, R., "Migration and Poverty," *Asia-Pacific Population Journal*, December 2002, pp. 67–82.

Srinivas, M.N, *The Remembered Village*, London: California, 1976.

Srinivas, M.N., *Social Change in Modern India*, Berkeley and Los Angeles: University of California Press, 1966.

Taylor, J.E., *The Migration of Labour*, Cambridge, Mass.: Harvard University Press, 1991.

Todaro, M.P., Internal Migration in Developing Countries, Geneva: ILO, 1976.

Tripathy, S.N., *Exploitation of Child Labour in Tribal India*, New Delhi: Daya Publishing House, 1991.

Verma, R.C., *Terror by Hunger*, New Delhi: Aravali Books International Pvt. Ltd., 2003

Visaria, P. and Basant, R., *Non-Agricultural Employment in India: Trends and Prospects*, New Delhi: Sage, 1993.

Vyas, N.N., *Bondage and Exploitation in Tribal India*, Delhi: Rawat Publications, 1980.

Walker, T.S. and J.G. Ryan, *Village and Household Economies in India's Semi-Arid Tropics*, Baltimore: Johns Hopkins, 1990.

Wiser, W. and C. Wiser, *Behind Mud Walls*, Berkeley: California, 1971.

Articles/Journals/Research Papers

Adams, J., "Studies of Indian Village Economies: A Bibliographic Essay.", *Indian Economic and Social History Review*, vol. 7, 1970a, pp. 109-137.

Anand, Vinod, "Poverty Syndrome: An Added Dimension of Concealed Poverty", *Mainstream*, vol. 40, no. 11, March 2, 2002, pp. 13-18.

Attwood, D.W., "Why Some of the Poor Get Richer: Economic Change and Mobility in Rural Western India.", *Current Anthropology*, vol. 20, no. 3, 1979. pp. 495-516.

Bardhan Pranab and Mookherjee Dilip, Political Economy of Land Reforms in West Bengal 1978-1998, June24, 2003.

Bardhan, Pranab, "Policy Issues and Less Developed Countries", *Economic Journal*, vol. 106, no. 438, September, 1996, pp. 1-56.

Battacharya, N. et al, "Changes in Level of Living in Rural West Bengal: Private Consumption", *Economic and Political Weekly,* July 11, 1987a.

Battacharya, N. et al, "Changes in Level of Living in Rural West Bengal: Social Consumption", *Economic and Political Weekly*, August 15, 1987b.

Battacharya, N. et al, "Changes in Level of Living in Rural West Bengal: Housing Conditions", *Economic and Political Weekly*, September 5-12, 1987d.

Battacharya, N. et al, "Changes in Level of Living in Rural West Bengal: Perceptions of the People.", *Economic and Political Weekly*. November 28, 1987e.

Besley Timothy and Burgess Robin, "Land Reform, Poverty Reduction, and Growth: Evidence from India," *Quarterly Journal of Economics*, vol. 15, no. 2, May 2000, pp. 389-430.

Besley, Timothy and Burgess, Robin, "Land Reform, Poverty Reduction and Growth: Evidence from India", *Quarterly Journal of Economics*, vol. 115, no. 2, May 2000, pp. 389-430.

Bhardan, P.K., 'The New Institutional Economics and Development Theory: A Brief Critical Assessment', World Development, vol. 17, no. 9, 1989, pp. 1389–95.

Bhowmik, P.K., "Occupational Changes in Two Villages in Bengal", *Man in India*, vol. 48, no. 1, January-March 1968, pp. 46-54.

Chakrapani, C. and Vijaya Kumar S., "Migration Pattern and Occupational Change (A Study of Palamur Labour in Andhra Pradesh," *The Indian Journal of Social Work*, vol. 55, no. 1, pp. 83–94;

Chattopadhyay, S.N., "Historical Context of Political Change in Rural West Bengal: A Study of Seven Villages in Bardhaman", *Economic and Political Weekly*, March 28, 1992.

Chaudhury Kalyan, "Bonded Labour", *Economic and Political Weekly*, Vol. 11, No. 11, 1976 pp. 415-16.

Chitnis, Govind K., "Is the Village Money Lender a Necessity?", *Rural India*, vol. 5, no. 9, September 1949, pp. 422-426.

Dandekar, V.M. and Rath, Nilakantha, "Poverty in India - I. Dimensions and Trends", *Economic and Political Weekly*, January 2, 1971.

Das, T.C., "Nature and Extent of Social Change in Tribal Society of Eastern India", *Sociological Bulletin*, vol. 11, nos.1-2, March-September 1962, pp. 221-238.

Datt, Gaurav and Ravallion, Martin, "Why Have Some Indian States Done Better in Reducing Rural Poverty?", *Economica*, vol. 65, no. 257, February, 1998, pp. 17-38.

Dent, Martin and Peters, Bill, "Poverty and Debt in Third World: Confronting Global Crisis", *Conflict Studies*, vol. 310, June-July, 1998, pp. 1-21.

Dev, S.M., "Pro-poor Growth in India: What do we know about the Employment Effects of Growth 1980–2000?" Working Paper 161, London: Overseas Development Institute, 2002.

Dowell, C. Mc. and De Haan, A., "Migration and Sustainable Livelihoods: a Critical Review of the Literature," *IDS Working Paper 65*, Brighton: Institute of Development Studies, University of Sussex, 1997

Dreze, Jean, Peter Lanjouw and Nareesh Sharma, "Economic Development 1957-1993," in Peter Lanjouw and Nicholas Stern,

Economic Development in Palanpur over Five Decades, Oxford: OUP, 1998.

Dubey, S.C. "Some Aspects of the Tribal Problem", *Eastern Anthropology*, vol. 3, no. 1, September 1949, pp. 28-35.

Duncan, Cynthia M., "Understanding Persistent Poverty: Social Class Context in Rural Communities", *Rural Sociology*, vol. 61, no. 1, Spring 1996, pp. 103-124.

Elizaga, Raquel Sosa, "Social Exclusion and Knowledge", *Current Sociology*, vol. 50, no. 1, January 2002, pp. 80-98.

Farrington, J., Christoplos, I., Kidd, A. with Beckman, M., "Extension, Poverty and

Fernandes, Walter, "Post-Independence Policies, Planned Development and Tribal Deprivation," in J.S. Bhandari and Subhadra Mitra Channa, *Tribes and Government Policies*, New Delhi: Cosmo Publications, 1997, p. 162.

Gadgil, Madhav, "Forest Management, Deforestation and People's Impoverishment", *Social Action*, vol. 39, no. 4, October-December 1989, pp. 357-383.

Gough, Kathleen, "Socio-Economic Change in Southeast India, 1950s to 1980s." *Journal of Contemporary Asia*, vol. 17, no. 3, 1987.

Gupta, Brij Gopal, "Rural Indebtedness", *Rural India*, vol. 15, no. 8, August 1952, pp. 286-288.

Gupta, S.P., "The Myth of Poverty Reduction", *India Today*, February 29, 1996.

Hirway, Indira, "Economic Growth, Rural Labour Markets in Poverty: Understanding the Linkages", *Indian Journal of Labour Economics,* vol. 38, no. 1, January-March, 1995, pp. 63-72.

Iqbal, F., "The Determinants of Moneylender Interest Rates: Evidence from Rural India", *Journal of Development Studies*, vol. 24. 1988.

Jodha, N.S., "Poverty Debate in India: A Minority view," *Economic and Political Weekly*, Special Number, November, 1988.

Kothari, U., 'Migration and Chronic Poverty', Working Paper 16, Manchester: Chronic Poverty Research Centre, Institute for Development Policy and Management, University of Manchester, 2002.

Kunal Sen & Ira N. Gang & Myeong-Su Yu , 2002. "Caste, Ethnicity and Poverty in Rural India," *IZA Discussion Papers 629*, Institute for the Study of Labour (IZA).

Kurien, C.T., "Dynamics of Rural Transformation: A Case Study of Tamil Nadu." *Economic and Political Weekly*, Annual Number, February 1980.

Lee, E.S., "A Theory of Migration," *Demography*, vol. 3, no. 1, 1966, pp. 47–57.

Lee, Steven, "Poverty and Violence", *Social Theory and Practice*, vol. 22, no. 1, Spring, 1996, pp. 67-82.

Lieten, "Poverty Alleviation Programmes: West Bengal's Experience", *Mainstream*, vol. 23, no. 35, June 2, 1991, pp. 21-25.

Mehta, B.H., "Forestry and Tensions in Tribal Areas", *Journal of Social Research*, Vol. 9, no. 2, September 1966, pp. 10-25.

Mehta, B.H., "Tribal Welfare and Forest Economy", *Journal of Social Research*, vol. 2, nos.1-2, March-September, 1959, pp. 72-81.

Mosse, D., Gupta, S., Mehta, M., V. Shah, Rees, J. and the KRIBP Project Team "Brokered Livelihoods: Debt, Labour Migration and Development in Tribal Western India," *Journal of Development Studies*, vol. 38, no. 5, June 2002, pp. 59–87.

Nancharaiah, G., "The Changing Position of Agricultural Labourers in the Labour Market", *Social Action*, vol. 40, no. 2, June 1990, pp. 172-183.

Olsen, W.K. and R.V. Ramana Murthy, "Contract Labour and Bondage in Andhra Pradesh (India)," *Journal of Social and Political Thought*, vol. 1, no. 2, June 2000.

Pal, Nirod Baran, "Socio-economic Perspective of a Land Reform Programme During left Front Government in West Bengal", *Teaching Politics*, vol. 17, nos.3-4, 1991, pp. 23-31.

Patnaik, K. Uma Shankar, "Poverty Levels, Consumptive Habits and Rural Welfare Schemes: An Inquiry into Pondicherry Beneficiaries", *Indian Journal of Economics*, vol. 81, no. 322, January 2001, pp. 341-360.

Pundlik, D.A., "The Problem of Rural Indebtedness" *Rural India*, vol. 12, no. 6, July 1949, pp. 289-292.

Ramchandran, V.K., "Land Reform Continues in West Bengal," http://www.pragoti.org/node/1875, 22 August 2008. Article courtesy *The Hindu.*

Ravallion, Martin and Gaurav Dutt, "Why has Economic Growth been more Pro-Poor in Some States of India than Others?", *Journal of Development Economics*, vol. 68, no. 2, August 2002, pp. 381-400.

Rogaly, B., Biswas, J., Coppard, D., Rafique, A., Rana, K. and Sengupta, A. 'Seasonal Migration, Social Change and Migrants Rights, Lessons from West Bengal', *Economic and Political Weekly*, 8 December: 4547–59.

Roy, Baren, "Tribal Problem in India", *Mainstream*, vol. 28, no. 13, January 20, 1990, pp. 28-30.

Sen, A., "Economic Reforms, Employment and Poverty: Trends and Options" *Economic and Political Weekly*, vol. 31, no. , 1996, pp. 35-37.

Sen, Arup Kumar, "Political Roots of Poverty", *Economic and Political Weekly*, vol. 35, no. 3, January 15-21, 2000, pp. 155-156.

Sinha, S.P., "Land Tenure, Ownership and Alienation in Bihar, West Bengal and Orissa," in S.N. Mishra(ed.), *Antiquity to Modernity in Tribal India Vol. III: Ownership and Control of the Resources among Indian Tribes*, New Delhi: Inter-India Publications, 1998, pp. 86-87.

Stark, V., "On the Role of Urban-Rural Remittances in Rural Development," *Journal of Development Studies*, vol. 16, no. 3, 1980, pp. 369–74.

Stevens, Ann Huff, "Climbing out of Poverty, Falling Back In: Measuring the Persistence of Poverty over Multiple Spells", *Journal of Human Resources*, vol. 34, no. 4, November 1999, pp. 557-588.

Unni, J., "Non-Agricultural Employment and Rural Livelihoods: Macro vis-a-vis Micro View", *The Indian Journal of Labour Economics*, vol. 39, no. 4, 1996, pp. 795-808.

Vulnerability: the Scope for Policy Reform: Final Report of a Study Conducted on Behalf of the Neuchâtel Initiative," *Working Paper 155*, London: Overseas Development Institute, 2001.

Vyas, V.S., "Farm and Non-farm Employment in Rural Areas: A Perspective for Planning." *Economic and Political Weekly*, vol. 34, no. 1, 1979.

Annexure 1

Final Report of Shri Arup Das, Hon'ble District Judge Purulia, 2000

In the Court
of
The Hon'ble Chief Justice Shri A.K.Mathur
And
The Hon'ble Justice Shri Barin Ghosh.

<u>In the matter of</u> :
W.P.No.3446(W) of 2000
PIL Case of Smt.Mahasveta Debi;

A N D

<u>In the matter of</u> :
Forwarding Letter No.5798-RG dt.4/5th September, 2000 of Shri Alak Kumar Basu, Registrar(General), High Court, Appellate Side, Calcutta, forwarding the direction of Your Lordships;

A N D

<u>In the matter of</u> :
Final report dated 10th November, 2000 of Arup Das, District Judge, Purulia.

With due respect I beg to submit the Final Report of Enquiry after visiting Kheria Sabar Pallies with 87 pages tour diary as follows:-

1). On 6-9-2000, I received the direction of Your

Lordships directing the District Judge, Purulia, to enquire and report on a) whether the tube-wells which have been sunk in 152 villages are still operating or not. How many of them are functioning and how many of them have gone out of use; b) whether the money which has been earmarked for repair of the tube-wells and wells have really been spent or not; c) with regard to the welfare schemes which have been implemented in various villages, the District Judge will make a sample check of some of the persons and find out whether Bank's subsidy given to the persons of the villages were really given or not.

2). On receiving the said directions I intimated the petitioner Smt.Mahasveta Debi and District Magistrate, Purulia. On 18-9-2000 Shri J.Dasgupta, District Magistrate-in-charge, Purulia, also met me.

I made it clear that one of the courts of the Additional District and Sessions Judge was lying vacant and another on the verge of retirement was expecting transfer at any moment, I could not leave Station ~~during~~ before the Puja vacation.

3). In consultation with Shri P.Rakshit and

Lordships directing the District Judge, Purulia, to enquire and report on a) whether the tube-wells which have been sunk in 152 villages are still operating or not. How many of them are functioning and how many of them have gone out of use; b) whether the money which has been earmarked for repair of the tube-wells and wells have really been spent or not; c) with regard to the welfare schemes which have been implemented in various villages, the District Judge will make a sample check of some of the persons and find out whether Bank's subsidy given to the persons of the villages were really given or not.

2). On receiving the said directions I intimated the petitioner Smt.Mahasveta Debi and District Magistrate, Purulia. On 18-9-2000 Shri J.Dasgupta, District Magistrate-in-charge, Purulia, also met me.

I made it clear that one of the courts of the Additiohal District and Sessions Judge was lying vacant and another on the verge of retirement was expecting transfer at any moment, I could not leave Station ~~during~~ before the Puja vacation.

3). In consultation with Shri P.Rakshit and

Shri P.Roy, Amicus curiae and on receiving tentative tour programme I intimated the same to the District Magistrate and Superintendent of Police, Purulia.

4). On receiving the permission of Your Lordships by Order dated 29-9-2000 to leave the Station, to use the official vehicle of the District Judge, Purulia, to purchase the fuel, to avoid audit enquiry and future complicity, I decided to visit Kheria Sabar Pallies avoiding the Puja days.

5). I visited 152 Sabar Pallies travelling 3853 km. on vehicle + travelling about 60 to 80 km. everyday and on occasion even upto 100 km. to reach first Sabar Pally starting from the District Judge's bungalow on and from 9-10-2000 to 11-10-2000 and 13-10-2000 to 25-10-2000 and 5-11-2000 plus walking almost 10 to 15 km. everyday except on 5-11-2000 visiting about 152 Sabar Pallies almost 95% of them are situated at far interior than the original villages. They prefer to live near the tank, Nala(ditch) or stream or river to avail water. I have gone through the Ails, uneven and rugged field, paddy-field, in between the bushes and jungle, hill, stepping down on the slope to cross the

the stream.

I crave leave to submit some pictures to show how I reached the Sabar Pallies.

6). I could not reach Ghalura inspite of going to the dense of the jungle on a hill very near to the Training Centre of M.C.C. (Naxalite- group) of Bihar, because I was prevented by the Chhotobabu of Bundwan P.S. being afraid of being ambushed in the event if I leave the vehicle and walk through the jungle about 50 minutes to reach the said Sabar Pally(P. 55 of tour diary).

7). I could not cross the Kumari river to reach Bhurrudih(I have taken a picture to show the inaccessibility of this Kumari river) and as there was no motorable road we could not go to the Sabar Pallies of Jonara, Pundru, Sasandih and Kashidih(Ghagra).

Due to increase of my blood pressure, I could not walk on the hill to reach Sirishgora. However, from Sirishgora, Shri Angad Sabar son of a freedom fighter Kanu Sabar and from Kashidih(Ghagra), two Sabars- Sanatan Sabar and Gurupada Sabar, met me and furnished the information.

I sincerely tender my apology for being unable to reach there.

8). Before my starting the enquiry, I received several telephones- a) threatening to involve me in contempt proceeding in connection with Bhadra Sabar's murder case(which is one of the root of the P.I.L. case), which has already been committed to my Court, Bidu alias Budhan Sabar's murder case which is pending for sanction as the C.B.I. has already been submitted charge-sheet and also to be committed to my Court and Hari Sabar's murder case which has already been committed to my court, b) informing that there would be resistance from the side of the vested interests to actual visit on some Sabar Pallies and to reveal the real picture.

9). I have annexed separate sheets showing the number of wells and tube-wells those have been sunk and how many of the wells are found usable or not usable and how many of the tube-wells are found functioning and not functioning. It will reveal a shocking picture that on several Sabar Pallies like Lotpada, a big village and Kuda with three other Sabar Tolas, there is no source of water.

In all I have found 90 wells are usable whereas 49 wells are not usable. 36 tube-wells are found functioning and 11 are not functioning.

a). No tube-well was found at village Akorbaid on 9-10-2000. I saw the marks of boring. It was bore in 1998(P.2 of tour diary). I have directed the petitioner's side to take a snap when I found a well-half-built, filled up with filthy water and worms to show the actual condition of the well and that I was discussing with S.A.E. about the reason why the well was not sunk properly.

b). Some wells are found not usable- filled up with trees and plants as at Nirvaipur, Kasidih, Golapara.

c). At Tilabani, I was told that from a tube-well worms are coming out during the month of Shravan. Here, I directed to pump the said tube-well and on two occasions, I found that muddy water was coming out(P.28 of tour diary).

d). At Kumari, one well, I was told, it was dug for the Sabars, but actually standing on the land of Jagannath Mahato(P.28 of tour diary).

e). At Chirudih one well was repaired only three days before my visit, but still not usable because of filthy water.

Needless to say that before my visit some wells have been constructed, some have been repaired and some tube-wells have been repaired which will be revealed from the annexure.

I crave leave to submit some pictures showing what I meant not-usable well and half-finished well and of some broken tube-wells.

10). In my tour-diary, I have already recorded that-

a). at Mairadih, one Sukdeb Sabar has received Rs.4500/- out of Rs.9000/-. He said that the rest was received by one <u>Atul Mahato</u>, not a Sabar.(P.3 of tour diary).

b). at Bankabali(Kenda), Bhadra Sabar received only Rs.200/-. He told that the sanction was for Rs.1200/-, one <u>Ardhendu Pal</u> took away the rest amount(P.6 of tour diary).

c). At Bansketya, Nunka Sabar has received Rs.2500/-. He has received a notice to repay the loan of Rs.6000/-(P.26 of tour diary).

d). at Fuljhore, Keshab has stated that he has received Rs.4766/- including the subsidy of Rs.2383/-, Bank loan- Rs.1430/- and actual loan- Rs.953/-. According to the paper, I saw that it was due to be paid with ten half-yearly instalments with interest, but he said that he actually got Rs.2200/-. The paper is annexed. (P.57 of tour diary).

e). at Chekua, Lalu Sabar said that he got only goat, but no loan.

f). at Ghagra Sabar Pally, <u>one lady called back</u> all the Sabars who gathered in front of me and <u>directed everyone not to talk</u>(P.58 of tour diary).

g). it was at Ghagra Sabar Pally where one Birati was found absent during the visit. Her son was present, but <u>prevented to talk</u>. One <u>Manke</u> told that Birati got Rs.1000/-. Shri P.Rakshit for the petitioner said that this Manke's father actually obtained the loan sanctioned for Birati with the help of Santal lady. Manke not being a Sabar, I scolded and prevented him from talking(P.58 of tour diary).

h). At Kheriadih I was told:"[illegible]", but the date was furnished to me that when they went to obtain the loan was 4-11-96(P.60 of tour diary).

i). at Adabona <u>village</u> where the Sabar Tola is actually situated at <u>Mouza</u> Gorasagma, I was told:"[illegible]", but nobody said about the amount of loan. Here, I saw a notice without mentioning date signed by Shri Ambujakshya

Mondal, Advocate, to Budhni Sabar, asking her to repay the loan of Rs.1575/-. She, however, claimed that as Budhu, she got Rs.800/- in hand. Here, I was specifically told : "[illegible]"(P.66 of tour diary).

j). at Jora-sal, Haralal claimed that although it has been recorded that he got Rs.1600/-, but actually he has got Rs.500/- in hand.

k). at Ja[illegible], Digambar Sabar told that he got a loan of Rs.5000/-, but after his withdrawal of the money, one Radhanath Mahato actually took away the money. Then said that Radhanath's son Baidyanath actually took away the money(P.63 of tour diary).

l). at Shyamnagar, Fulmani said : "[illegible]"(P.64 of tour diary).

m). at Kandowa, I saw a notice issued from Mallabhum Gramin Bank, Barabazar Branch, being No.249 dated 3-3-98 in respect of the loan for Rs.1320/- and the notice was for Rs.2354/- with interest.

n). I have annexed separate sheet showing what they obtained as a loan which I ascertained from the Sabars. In many occasions, I found that non-Sabars were trying to speak instead of Sabar with a view to mislead the enquiry.

o). In most of the occasions, I found that the Sabars who actually got the loan mysteriously absent just at the time of my visit. I have the impression that for whatever reasons Sabars have been threatened that immediately after my visit, they would be forced to repay the loan. I have also the impression that in many occasions, the Sabars have said that somebody have got loan, but the amount of the loan was denied by other Sabars. Somebody said that they received loan 4/5/6/7 thousand rupees.

11). I was shocked to see that some rocky lands have been given to the Sabars as Patta which are not cultivable. For this reason, I felt that a video recording will actually reveal what kind of land that has been given to the Sabar as Patta. Almost everywhere Patta-papers were given to the Sabars, but not the land. In many occasions, I was told that Patta-papers were taken away from the Sabars. Therefore, I can not mention in my report the number of Patta Plots. It can easily be challenged.

a). At Bengthupi, in all, 14 Sabars have got Pattas. They were forced to work as <u>day-labourers</u>. The Sabars said that <u>only with the help of Kenda P.S.</u>, they are cultivating the land only for the last two years(P.5 of tour diary).

b). At Nirvaipur in 30 decimals of land, 52 Sabars have been granted Pattas. No one, but Buru Sabar has got the land. He cultivates 0.49

acres of land(P.10 of tour diary).

c). At Kasidih, in all, 20 Sabar-families have been granted 60 Bighas of land, but they are not in possession. After one occasion, they have been dispossessed. At present other villagers are cultivating those lands(P.11 of tour diary).

d). At Makarkendi, in all, 15 Sabars have got Pattas but except Charan Sabar nobody has got the land. Charan is cultivating .03 acres of land.

e). At Raherdih(Maguria), Pattas have been issued for three acres of land to 13 Sabar-families, but none has got land.

f). At Sargo, six Sabars have got Pattas, but not possession. Amongst them, Binode and Chhutulal have got their lands below the river belt.

g). At Gohmikocha, Pattas have been granted to Jogindra, Pashupati and Gurucharan. They are cultivating their lands partly. Pattas were taken away by Gram Panchayet without identifying the lands for the rests.(P.22 of tour-diary).

h). At Latpada, 12/14 Sabars have got Pattas, but no land. Whatever were given to them are said to be Dungri. Even, not properly identified.

i). At Bansketya, in all eight Sabars have got Pattas and lands. All the papers are lying with Ex-pradhan, Thakurdas Murmu(P.26 of tour diary).

j). At Kalipur, all have got Pattas. All were cultivating their lands. Since C.A.D.C. has taken over their lands now they can not cultivate. C.A.D.C. has not yet paid full compensation, but they are providing some works. Here, they are drinking water from their old-Colony(P.72 of tour-diary).

k). At Kandowa, the Patta-lands of Pashupati, Ratan and Signa have been taken over by the said C.A.D.C. Therefore, they are not cultivating their lands. They do not know whether subsequently any land has been provided or not.

l). At Banddih, Buka,Majhi Sabar, Ananda and Fulchand have got Patta-papers, but not possession of land. They said :"[illegible]".

Same is the position of another Sabar Tola Bandhkuli where no land has been demarcated.

m). At Sirga also, the Sabars have got Patta-papers, but they could not cultivate because they were identified Danga-lands.

n). At Bhaspara, Pattas have been granted for 0.05 acres in Plot No.139 for six Sabars, but one Nagen Mudi has taken away four of the Patta-papers. (P.25 of tour Diary)

o). At Kelardih Pattas have been granted in favour of three Sabars, but actual place is a place of worship known as "Joyer Than". (P.26 of tour diary)

p). At Kumari Sabar-tola one teacher has been threatened for writing to the authority which according to the Sabars ultimate causing my visit. Therefore, they did not disclose about their Patta-lands or loans.

q). At Beldih, I was told that J.L.No.97, Plot No.789, area 45 decimals and Plot No.924 area 81 decimals of lands were given Patta to Dibakar Sabar. Those lands were taken over by Purulia Phosphate without paying any compensation.

r). At Adabana village where the Sabar-tola is situated at mouza Gorasagma, Kitu Sabar has got Patta-land where one Brindaban Sadhu(Mahato) has built his Ashram. Therefore, depriving Kitu Sabar from Possession of his land(P.70 of tour diary).

s). At Bikramdih, Sabars are cultivating Babui, but for last two years, they are prevented from collecting Babui for the purpose of making rope by <u>Kalipada and Muchiram Mahato</u>. (P.64 of tour-diary).

I crave leave to submit some pictures to show the actual condition of the Patta-lands.

12). In respect of Ghars built under 'Indira Abas Yojana', I found-

a). At Balakdih, 19 Ghars were built without tiles. They collapsed about 10/15 years ago.

b). At Makarkendi out of 11 Ghars only two were found existing.

c). At Bansketya, Ghars were built in the year 1977-78. All collapsed.

d). At Chirugora, 9 Ghars were built 3/4 years ago, but collapsed <u>within 15 days after construction</u>. The Audit Officer, who was then accompanying me, <u>admitted</u> that <u>without checking the actual</u> condition of the Ghars bills were passed(page-30 of tour diary).

e). At Chitaghata and Penchara, the Ghars have been built <u>without window</u>.

f). At Haludbana, Ghars have been built without <u>window and door</u>. Here, I found that Rabani's Ghar that has been built this year, but has been collapsed.

g). At Gurur, Ghars have been built only <u>fifteen days</u> before my visit.

h). At Chila, one Ghar has been built for Gurucharan. From outside, it looked very well, but inside unfinished.

i). At Kalipur one Ghar with brick-wall and cemented roof has been built accommodating six families in that house. Water percolates from the roof. Rooms are all dark. One month ago, C.A.D.C. authority built privy without door without pan(picture is annexed) [P.72 of tour-diary].

13). Bandh:-

a). At Suala, a Bandh has been built measuring 50' x 50' x 12', but not yet ready for cultivation. It has been built by Block. The Sabars have reported that out of Rs.40000/-, the Block has spent actually Rs.29000/-.

b). At Kasidih, a Bandh has been sanctioned for the Sabars, but actually it has been excavated in the land of Amulya Singh Sardar.

c). At Sargo, Gram Panchayet has constructed a tank for which a sum of Rs.50000/- has been allotted. But, I was told that the work was actually done for Rs.10000/-. The work has been stopped for about three months. I was also told that on two occasions, Gram Panchayat has constructed this tank.

d). At Gohmikocha, Gram Panchayat has paid Rs.20000/- out of Rs.30000/- for construction of a Bandh in the <u>month of January, 2000</u>.

e). At Daldaria, this year a Bandh has been built at Rs.50000/-.

f). At Fuljhore, one Bandh has been sanctioned for the Sabars, but <u>actually has been excavated in the land of Santal</u>.

g). At Bhalukdih, 5 Hapas(small-tank) have been constructed, but <u>without any water</u>.

h). At Kashipur, on the land of Sahadeb Sabar a Bandh has been excavated for which on two occasions money has been spent Rs.15000/- + Rs.20000/- = Rs.35000/-.

14). At Pitidiri, 10 H.P.water-pump has been allotted in favour of Sabars. But, actually it is now kept by one <u>Biswanath Mahato</u>. Therefore, Sabars are depriving from using this water-pump(P.35 of tour diary).

At Jaira, one water-pump-set has been allotted for the Sabars, but <u>without giving any pipe</u>. It is not working for four years(P.36 of tour-diary).

15). At Pitidiri during the visit I find that fifteen days ago, one hostel has been constructed for the Sabars <u>without doors and windows</u>.

16). At Kelardih, three Sabars were granted Pattas in a place of worship "Joyer Than".

I crave leave to submit a picture of this "Joyer Than".

I was told that if the Sabars would try to possess this land, there would be a clash in between the Sabar community and Santal community.

17). My Tour-Diary will reveal that although I left Harbana at 2.50 p.m., but as I could complete the day's programme on 13-10-2000, I went to Kuda where I could not reach on 10-10-2000. On 13-10-2000, I could reach Kuda at 4.20 p.m. On the way I halted at Turung, another Sabar Pally at 4.30 p.m. Similarly, on 16-10-2000, where I could reach I visited the places and completed the day's work upto 5 p.m. and at Chila on 19-10-2000, I visited the place even upto 5.20 p.m. Therefore, to conclude the visit, I tried my level best to reach all the Sabar Pallies, but where I could not reach due to inaccessibility, I have mentioned in my Tour Diary. At Ghalura, I could not reach being afraid of being ambushed in a jungle of a hill.

18). I went to Chekua where I saw the Sabars

and Santals were taking position on the trees with their bows and arrows to tackle five of the forty-two Dalma elephants, those were coming down from the otherside of the hill. Here, we literally ran away from the village.

19). The worst that I have found that at Amjharna almost all male Sabars fled away being nude having nothing to wear even after fifty years of independence. Even a husband and wife who had something to cover could not stand up. Here, Kheria-Sabars Kalyan Samity sent some clothings before my visit(P.7 of tour-diary). Shri P.Rakshit later on admitted that even in this place for the purpose of this visit for the first time, he could reach.

In anticipation of Your Lordships' permission to make my report truthful on and from 16-10-2000 I have permitted Shri Amitabha Mukherjee, an amateur, to take picture on his video. Occasionally only I directed him to take picture to show the condition of wells, tube-wells and Ghars under 'Indira Abas Yojana'. In fact, he has no idea as for the purpose of this visit. The correspondents from "Purulia Darpan", who accompanied the petitioners side was permitted to take my interview to make this audio-pictures meaningful.

I crave leave to enclose annexures:-

1). One for the wells and tube-wells.

2). For the loan obtained by Sabars.

3). Some papers that were given from the Kheria Sabar Samity to show the notices that I have mentioned and Patta-papers to show what lands were granted to the Sabars.

4). The report of the District Magistrate, Purulia, and B.D.Os. submitted to me before this visit.

I tender my apology that out of fear and sabotage, blood-pressure, shaking of hand, I maintained the field-books in a very cryptic manner obtaining some signatures even from a child to show that actually I went there which will also be reflected from some of the pictures that I am submitting along with my report and the uncensored copy of the video photographs for which I have paid the money to purchase the pictures. I have mentioned some page numbers from tour diary for ready reference. Under lines are mine

Yours faithfully,

Arup Das
(Arup Das),
District Judge, Purulia.
10.11.2000

Annexure 2

Affidavit of the Chief Secretary to the Government of West Bengal, 2002 and Five Continuous Pages form the List of Land Allocation to the Tribals

DISTRICT : PURULIA

IN THE HIGH COURT AT CALCUTTA
CONSTITUTIONAL WRIT JURISDICTION
APPELLATE SIDE

W. P. No. 3446 (W) of 2000

In the Matter of :

Letter Written by Maheswata Devi.

AFFIDAVIT AFFIRMED BY CHIEF SECRETARY TO THE GOVERNMENT OF WEST BENGAL PURSUANT TO ORDER DATED FEBRUARY 22, 2002 PASSED BY THIS HON'BLE COURT.

I, S. N. Ray . Son of aged about 57 Years, by faith Hindu having office at Writer's Building . Kolkata 700001 do hereby solemnly affirm and say as follows :-

1. That I am the chief secretary to the Govt of W.Bengal as such well conversant with the facts and circumstances of the instant case.

2. That I have gone through the Writ Petition and all annexures thereto as also a copy of the report dated November 5, 2000 submitted by the Learned District Judge Purulia, before this Hon'ble Court and I have understood the contents and purport thereof. I am comptent to

affirm this Affidavit. In pursuance of the Order dated February 22, 2002 I crave leave of this Hon'ble Court to report the status of the development works undertaken by the State Government for Kheria Sabar Community in the District of Purulia as also steps taken against the persons responsible for misappropriation of the funds.

3. In compliance with the direction of this Hon'ble Court upon the Chief Secretary Government of West Bengal, interalia, to look into any commission or ommission on te part of persons or bodies in implementing the developmental and welfare activities for the Kheria Sabar Community and to indentify the erring official/ bodies / Panchayat functioneries and to fix responsibilities upon them, a Committee headed by the District Magistrate, Purulia, has been constituted as per order issued under Memo No. 8/CS-2001 dated January 3, 2002.

4. a) Thereafter, the District Magistrate Purulia formed four groups from amoggst the members of the aforesaid Committee as follows to look into the cases pointed out by the Learned District Judge,Purulia .

(i) Construction of huts and excavation/re-excavation of bundhs/tanks/Hapas(small tanks)

(ii) Condition & Tube Wells / Wells.

(iii) Distribution and possession and Vested lands.

The above mentioned four groups undertook visits of the localities on and from January 20, 2001 and submitted report on the observation of Learned District Judge, Purulia. The District Magistate on receipt of aforesaid report issued instruction and directions to the concerned applicants who seemed to be respondible for commission and ommission leading to non implementation of develooment and welfare activities and embezzement of Government money meant for the development of Sabar Community.

5. Thereafter the State Administratiue at the District level headed by District Magistrate, Purulia took the following actions.

(i) Departmental proceeding started against the Officials.

(ii) Resume of action regarding the land related irregulaties, and omission and commissions by various Government official and Panchayat functioneries.

(iii) Regarding institutional action for violation of Government Procedure in respect of Government sponsored Schemes.

(iv) Development works under taken upto March 18, 2002.

The District Magistrate, Purulia thereafter, submited his report dated March 20, 2002 in the above matter annexing the documents and papers related thereto.

(b) The aforesaid report dated March, 20,

2002 is annexed hereto with its all annexures and marked with Letter

'R1' 'R1'.

6. It is humbly submitted that the Chief Secretary, Government of West Bengal have complied with the Order dated December 8, 2000 with utmost sincerity and the process of penal measures against the erring official as also the continuous process of development work of the Kheria Sabar Community has been under his active consideration and close scrutiny in co-ordination with the Government functioneries at different levels.

7. Statements made in Paragraphs 1 (one) to 4 (four), 5 (b) are true to my knowledge and those made in 5(a) .... paragraphs are based on information derived from records which I verily believe to be true and the rest are my humble submission before this Hon'ble Court.

Prepared in my Office

Sd. Samrath De

Advocate.

The deponent is known to me

Clerk to :

Mr.

Advocate

Solemnly affirmed before me

on this day of April,

2002.

COMMISSIONER.

Name of the Block	Name of the Mouza With J.L No.	Name of the Sabar Pattadars	Vested Land alloted			R.S case No.	Nature of the land	Remarks
			R.S plot No.	Area in acres	Classification			
BANDWAN	BURUHOR-128	98.Naru Sabar s/o Dhunda	74 695	0.13 0.67	Danga Gora		Uncultivable Uncultivable	
		99.Sambhu Sabar s/o Robi	751	0.82	Danga		Uncultivable	
		100.Kalu Sabar s/o Robi	751	0.83	Danga		Uncultivable	
		101.Sufal Sabar s/o Budhu	60 102 313 552	[illegible] [illegible] [illegible] 0.21	M.Ail Danga Danga Danga		Uncultivable Uncultivable Uncultivable Uncultivable	
		102.Birsingh Sabar s/o Budhu	571 924	0.59 [illegible]	Danga Danga		Uncultivable Uncultivable	
		103.Kuchi Sabar s/o Budhu	895	0.90	Danga		Uncultivable	
		104.Buka Sabar s/o Baneswar	895	0.90	Danga		Uncultivable	
		105.Bisnu Sabar s/o Baneswar	895	0.78	Danga		Uncultivable	
		106.Gandhu Sabar s/o Baneswar	954	0.90	Danga		Uncultivable	
		107.Sadhu Sabar s/o Baneswar	954	0.90	Danga		Uncultivable	
		108.Hajal Sabar s/o Sahan	954 959 754	0.45 0.14 0.04	Danga Danga M.Ail		Uncultivable Uncultivable Uncultivable	
		109.Jaganath Sabar s/o Sahan	583	0.78	Danga		Uncultivable	
		110.Ghuna Sabar s/o Guhiram	959	0.80	Danga		Uncultivable	
		111.Paul Sabar s/o Guhiram	959	0.80	Danga		Uncultivable	
		112.Budhu Sabar s/o Luka	959 140	0.39 0.26	Danga Gora		Uncultivable Uncultivable	
		113.Rabi Sabar s/o Luka	959 141 772	0.20 0.04 0.46	Danga Gora Gora		Uncultivable Uncultivable Uncultivable	

Name of the Block	Name of the Mouza With J.L No.	Name of the Sabar Pattadars	Vested Land alloted			R.S case No.	Nature of the land	Remarks
			R.S plot No.	Area in acres	Classification			
BANDWAN	BURDHOR-128	114.Guhiram Sabar s/o	98	2.00	Danga		Uncultivable	
		115.Dhunda ram Sabar s/o	98 95 87 72	0.86 0.85 0.24 0.05	Danga Danga Danga Danga		Uncultivable Uncultivable Uncultivable Uncultivable	
		116.Kanai Sabar s/o	122 148	0.80 1.00	Gora Danga.		Uncultivable Uncultivable	
		117.Sahan Sabar s/o	148 648 305 617	1.00 0.34 0.04 0.37	Danga Gora Baid Danga		Uncultivable Uncultivable Cultivable Uncultivable	
		118.[illegible]war Sabar s/o	148 163 571	1.07 0.[illegible] 0.5[illegible]	Danga Baid Danga		Uncultivable Cultivable Uncultivable	
		119.Burtheswar Sabar s/o	15[illegible]	1.7[illegible]	Gora		Uncultivable	
		120.Rabi sabar s/o	158	1.[illegible]	Gora		Uncultivable	
		121.Digam Sabar s/o	158	1.5[illegible]	Gora		Uncultivable	
		122.Chakla Sabar s/o Bharat	969 12[illegible]	[illegible] 0.05	Danga Danga		Uncultivable Uncultivable	
		123.Ludhu Sabar s/o Chand	725 722	0.63 0.38	Gora Danga		Uncultivable Uncultivable	
		124.Bhaga Sabar s/o Guman	313	1.00	Danga		Uncultivable	
	GURUR – 05	125.Suchand Sabar s/o Jaganath	2754	0.22	Gora	1/85 dt 2.7.85	Uncultivable	
		126.Sahan Sabar s/o Jogen	2754	0.22	Gora	Do	Uncultivable	
		127.Rohin Sabar s/o Bej	2754	0.22	Gora	Do	Uncultivable	
		128.Anil Sabar s/o Robi	2754	0.22	Gora	Do	Uncultivable	
		129.Kesab Sabar s/o Budhu	2754	0.22	Gora	Do	Uncultivable	

Name of the Block	Name of the Mouza With J.L No.	Name of the Sabar Pattadars	Vested Land alloted			R.S case No.	Nature of the land	Remarks
			R.S plot No.	Area in acres	Classification			
BANDWAN	GURUR – 05	130.Gayaram Sabar s/o Suchand	2754	0.21	Gora	1/85 dt 2.7.85	Uncultivable	
		131.Manu Sabar s/o Suchand	2754	0.21	Gora	Do	Uncultivable	
		132.Joyti Sabar s/o Suchand	2754	0.21	Gora	Do	Uncultivable	
		133.Raju Sabar s/o Suchand	2754	0.21	Gora.	Do	Uncultivable	
		134.Puita Sabar s/o Maria	1198/1247 242 33	1.00 1.25 0.54	Danga Danga Gora	8/82-83	Uncultivable Uncultivable Uncultivable	
		135.Chuta Sabar s/o Maria	1198/1247 426	0.34 0.66	Danga Danga	12/72-73 dt 4.5.73	Uncultivable Uncultivable	
		136.Dhabani Sabar s/o Maria	426	1.00	Danga	Do	Uncultivable	
		137.Kala Sabar s/o Kedar	1044	1.00	Danga	Do	Uncultivable	
		138.Laga Sabar s/o Kandru	1044 542 442 818 1555 962	0.03 0.51 0.12 0.12 [illegible] 0.03	Danga Danga Danga Danga Danga Danga	Do Do Do Do Do Do	Uncultivable Uncultivable Uncultivable Uncultivable Uncultivable Uncultivable	
		139.Mara Sabar s/o Maria	253 259 281 433 268 77 341	0.01 0.02 0.26 0.18 0.30 0.21 0.01	Danga Danga Danga Danga Danga Danga Danga	Do Do Do Do Do Do Do	Uncultivable Uncultivable Uncultivable Uncultivable Uncultivable Uncultivable Uncultivable	
		140.Chuka Sabar s/o Maria	426 1044	0.28 0.72	Danga Danga	Do Do	Uncultivable Uncultivable	
	PARGORA-88	141.Leda Sabar s/o Lakhiram	33 34 317 254 292	0.22 0.16 0.16 0.41 0.70	Baid Baid Gora Gora Gora	2/72-7 do do do do	Cultivable Cultivable Uncultivable Uncultivable Uncultivable	

Name of the Block	Name of the Mouza With J.L No.	Name of the Sabar Pattadars	Vested and alloted			R.S case No.	Nature of the land	Remarks
			R.S plot No.	Area in acres	Classification			
BANDWAN	PARGORA-88	142.Samala	292	1.00	Gora	2/72-73	Uncultivable	
		Sabar	392	0.16	Gora	do	Uncultivable	
		s/o-Kala	394	0.20	Gora	do	Uncultivable	
			395	0.20	Kanali	do	Cultivable	
			397	0.12	Baid	do	Cultivable	
		143.Dhunda	378	0.35	Baid	Do	Cultivable	
		Sabar	16/382	0.13	Bastu	Do	Homestead	Homestead
		s/o Gopal	391	0.50	Kanali	Do	Cultivable	
			402	0.08	Gora	Do	Uncultivable	
			408	0.10	Baid	Do	Cultivable	
			410	0.20	Baid	Do	Cultivable	
			132/411	0.16	[illegible]hal	Do	Cultivabel	
		144.Suku Sabar	390	0.35	Kanali	Do	Cultivable	
		s/o [illegible]kiram	391	0.50	Kanali	Do	Cultivable	
			124	0.50	Gora	Do	Uncultivable	
			122	0.09	Gora	Do	Uncultivable	
	BANGRI(JARAGORA)-102	145.Bayan Sabar s/o Mangal	421	1.00	Danga	7/1983 dt [illegible].7.83	Uncultivable	
		146.Bistu Sabar s/o Mangal	421	1.00	Danga	Do	Uncultivable	
		147.Lakhiram Sabar s/o Maru	421	1.00	Danga	Do	Uncultivable	
		148.Bharat Sabar s/o Satrughan	421	1.00	Danga	Do	Uncultivable	
		149.Shankar Sabar s/o Satrughan	421	1.00	Danga	Do	Uncultivable	
		150.Behari	479	0.50	Danga	Do	Uncultivable	
		Sabar s/o Satrughan	454	0.50	Danga	Do	Uncultivable	
		151.Ram Sabar	382	0.54	Danga	Do	Uncultivable	
		s/o	30	0.25	Baid	Do	Cultivable	
		Barashambhu	421	0.20	Danga	Do	Uncultivable	

Name of the Block	Name of the Mouza With J.L No.	Name of the Sabar Pattadars	Vested Land alloted			R.S case No.	Nature of the land	Remarks
			R.S plot No.	Area in acres	Classification			
BANDWAN	BANGRI(JARAGORA) 102	152.Dalu Sabar s/o Maha	343 32 33 24 21	0.44 0.07 0.01 0.04 0.04	Gora Baid Gora Danga Danga	2/1983 dt 19.7.83	Uncultivable Cultivable Uncultivable Uncultivable Uncultivable	
		153.Nitai Sabar s/o Naran	526 527 525 461	0.12 0.51 0.09 0.27	M.Ail Baid M.Ail Danga	Do Do Do Do	Uncultivable Cultivable Uncultivable Uncultivable	
	KARRU - 127	154.Budhu Sabar s/o Bura	144 1102 229	0.40 0.04 0.17	Gora M. Ail Gora	3/82-83 do do	Uncultivable Uncultivable Uncultivable	
		155.Sudhir Sabar s/o Dhana	219 1091	0.33 0.04	Gora M.Ail	Do Do Do	Uncultivable Uncultivable	
		156.Fakir Sabar s/o Shyam	1127	0.50	Gora	Do Do	Uncultivable	
		157.Gura Sabar s/o Dharam	1127	0.50	Gora	Do Do	Uncultivable	
		158.Gobinda Sabar s/o Kartik	1127	0.50	Gora	Do	Uncultivable	
		159.Kala Sabar s/o Mahadeb	1127	0.50	Gora	Do	Uncultivable	
		160.Runga Sabar s/o Mangal	1127	0.50	Gora	Do	Uncultivable	
		161.Mathan Sabar s/o Sanatan	1127	0.41	Gora	Do	Uncultivable	
		162.Manu Sabar s/o Robi	1144	0.50	Gora	Do	Uncultivable	
	YASHPUR – 76	163.Mariram Sabar s/o Mangal	997 789 372 349	0.20 0.28 0.02 0.04	Bahal Gora Danga Danga	Do	Cultivable Uncultivable Uncultivable Uncultivable	
		164.Sanatan Sabar s/o Joyram	533 789 346 453	0.20 0.27 0.01 0.02	Bahal Gora Danga Danga	Do	Cultivable Uncultivable Uncultivable Uncultivable	

Annexure 3

List of Pending Cases Lodged by the Tribals during 2005

গ্রামীণ কর্মনিশ্চয়তা আইন ২০০৫, অভিযোগের তালিকা

জেলা - পুরুলিয়া

ক্রমিক নং	অভিযোগ	অভিযোগকারী	কাকে অভিযোগ জানানো হয়েছে	গ্রাম পঞ্চায়েত	ব্লক	ব্যবস্থা কি নেওয়া হয়েছে
১.	বেকার ভাতা না দেওয়া।	সন্তোষ মাঝি সহ [illegible] জন।	বি. ডি. ও	[illegible]	মানবাজার	
২.	কাজ না দেওয়া।	[illegible] সহ ৫৪ জন।	বিডিও	পুঞ্চা	পুঞ্চা	
৩.	বেকার ভাতা না দেওয়া	সুধীর কুমার মুর্মু সহ ৪৮ জন।	পঞ্চায়েত প্রধান	ইন্দারা, বাঁধগোড়া, গোঁড়াশোল	মানবাজার	
৪.	কাজের তথ্য ইস্যুকার্ড না দেওয়া / মজুরি [illegible]	ললিত সিং সহ ১০ জন।	পঞ্চায়েত প্রধান	ইন্দারা	মানবাজার।	
৫.	বেকার ভাতা না দেওয়া	অমূল্য ঘোষ সহ ৫২ জন।	বি. ডি. ও	বেলা	বলরামপুর	
৬.	কাজ না দেওয়া।	কালিপদ ঘোষ সহ ১১ জন।	পঞ্চায়েত প্রধান ও বি. ডি. ও.	বেলা	বলরামপুর	
৭.	কাজ না দেওয়া।	সন্তোষ মাহাত সহ ২০ জন।	পঞ্চায়েত প্রধান ও বি. ডি. ও	বেলা.	বলরামপুর।	
৮.	কাজ না দেওয়া.	রমাকান্ত ঘোষ সহ ৯ জন	প্রধান ও বি. ডি. ও	বেলা	বলরামপুর।	
৯.	কাজ না দেওয়া।	জগৎ সিং সর্দার সহ ১২ জন।	পঞ্চায়েত প্রধান ও বি. ডি. ও	বেলা	বলরামপুর।	
১০.	কাজ না দেওয়া।	[illegible] সিং সর্দার সহ ৫ জন।	পঞ্চায়েত প্রধান ও বি. ডি. ও	বেলা	বলরামপুর।	

গ্রামীণ কর্মনিশ্চয়তা আইন ২০০৫, অভিযোগের তালিকা

জেলা : পুরুলিয়া

ক্রমিক নং	অভিযোগ	অভিযোগকারী	কাকে অভিযোগ জানানো হয়েছে	গ্রাম পঞ্চায়েত	ব্লক	ব্যবস্থা কি নেওয়া হয়েছে
১১.	কাজ না দেওয়া।	প্রেস্কা মাহাত সহ ৫২ জন	পঞ্চায়েত প্রধান ও বিডিও	পুঞ্চা	পুঞ্চা	
১২.	জব কার্ড না দেওয়া	রাজু সর্দার সহ ১৬ জন,	বি.ডি.ও	পুঞ্চা	পুঞ্চা	
১৩.	জব কার্ড না দেওয়া.	জালেশ্বর কিস্কু সহ ১৯ জন।	বি.ডি.ও	চিরুডি	হুড়া	
১৪.	কাজের তথ্য সংক্রান্ত বোর্ডে নোটিশ না টাঙানো।	অশ্বিনী সিং সর্দার সহ 22জন।	বিডিও	বেলা	বলরামপুর।	
১৫.	কাজ না দেওয়া।	জহরলাল মাহাত সহ ১৮ জন।	প্রধান ও বি.ডি.ও	লাখড়া	পুঞ্চা।	
১৬.	কাজ না দেওয়া।	সরস্বতী মাহাত সহ 20 জন।	বি.ডি.ও	লাখড়া	পুঞ্চা।	
১৭.	কাজ না দেওয়া।	প্রবোধ মাহাত সহ 28 জন.	বি.ডি.ও.	বাগদা.	পুঞ্চা।	
১৮.	কাজ না দেওয়া.	সুমিত্রা মাহাত সহ ১৩২ জন	বি.ডি.ও	পুঞ্চা	পুঞ্চা.	
১৯.	কাজ না দেওয়া	নিতাই মাঝি সহ ৬৮ জন,	বি.ডি.ও	কুচিয়া	মানবাজার	
২০.	কাজ না দেওয়া।	রঞ্জিত গোপ সহ ৪৩ জন।	বি.ডি.ও	বড়রা	পুঞ্চা।	

গ্রামীণ কর্মনিশ্চয়তা আইন ২০০৫, অভিযোগের তালিকা

জেলা — পুরুলিয়া

ক্রমিক নং	অভিযোগ	অভিযোগকারী	কাকে অভিযোগ জানানো হয়েছে	গ্রাম পঞ্চায়েত	ব্লক	ব্যবস্থা কি নেওয়া হয়েছে
২১.	কাজ না দেওয়া	কালি টুডু সহ ৩৭ জন।	প্রধান (পঞ্চায়েত)	গড়শিকা	সাঁতুড়ি	
২২.	কাজ না দেওয়া	জয়ন্তী ঘোষ সহ ৭৩ জন।	পঞ্চায়েত প্রধান	ভেলা	বলরামপুর	
২৩.	কাজ না দেওয়া	রতন মোহন সহ ২. জন।	পঞ্চায়েত প্রধান	চাঁড়ালগড়ি	সাঁতুড়ি।	
২৪.	কাজ না দেওয়া	জমিল টুডু সহ ৮ জন।	বি.ডি.ও	চাঁড়ালগড়ি	সাঁতুড়ি।	
২৫.	কাজ না দেওয়া	চাঁদমনি মুর্মু	বি. ডি.ও.	কেশরপুর	সাঁতুড়ি।	
২৬.	কাজ না দেওয়া	আনন্দ বাউড়ি সহ ২৩৮ জন।	বি.ডি.ও	চিড়কিডি	হুড়া।	
২৭.	কাজ না দেওয়া।	ভীম সর্দার সহ ৭ জন।	বি.ডি.ও	বাসদা	পুঞ্চা।	
২৮.	কাজ না দেওয়া।	সুজিতকুমার মেমপ্রম সহ ১৪ জন।	বি.ডি.ও	বিশ্বরী	মানবাজার-১	
২৯.	কাজের তথ্য সংক্রান্ত বিষয়ে নোটিশ বোর্ডে না টাঙানো।	নারুগোপাল মাহাত	বি.ডি.ও	লাখড়া	পুঞ্চা।	
৩০.	বেকারভাতা না দেওয়া।	প্রবৃতি মাহাত সহ ১৭ জন।	বি.ডি.ও	লাখড়া	পুঞ্চা।	

গ্রামীণ কর্মনিশ্চয়তা আইন ২০০৫, অভিযোগের তালিকা

জেলা - পুরুলিয়া

ক্রমিক নং	অভিযোগ	অভিযোগকারী	কাকে অভিযোগ জানানো হয়েছে	গ্রাম পঞ্চায়েত	ব্লক	ব্যবস্থা কি নেওয়া হয়েছে
৩১.	বেকার ভাতা না দেওয়া.	শংকর বেসরা	বি.ডি.ও	বিশড়ি	মানবাজার-১নং	
৩২.	বেকার ভাতা না দেওয়া.	মানাকুর মান্ডি সহ ৩২ জন।	বি.ডি.ও	মোড়লবাড়ি	সাঁতুড়ি।	
৩৩.	বেকার ভাতা না দেওয়া	বিনোদ বেসরা সহ ৯ জন।	বি.ডি.ও	ডাঁড়াবাড়ি	সাঁতুড়ি।	
৩৪.	বেকার ভাতা না দেওয়া.	লক্ষণ মাহাত সহ ২৬ জন।	বি.ডি.ও	গড়শিকা.	সাঁতুড়ি।	
৩৫.	বেকার ভাতা না দেওয়া	জিতু মুর্মু সহ ২৪ জন।	বি.ডি.ও	ডাঁড়াবাড়ি	সাঁতুড়ি।	
৩৬.	বেকার ভাতা না দেওয়া.	জিতু মুর্মু সহ ১২ জন।	বি.ডি.ও	ডাঁড়াবাড়ি	সাঁতুড়ি।	
৩৭.	বেকার ভাতা না দেওয়া.	বরুণ মান্ডি সহ ৯ জন।	বি.ডি.ও	ডাঁড়াবাড়ি	সাঁতুড়ি।	
৩৮.	বেকার ভাতা না দেওয়া	বসন্তকুমার সিংহ সহ 20 জন।	বি.ডি.ও	নপাড়া	পুঞ্চা।	
৩৯.	বেকার ভাতা না দেওয়া.	বসন্তকুমার সিংহ সহ ৫ জন।	বি.ডি.ও	নপাড়া	পুঞ্চা.	
৪০.	বেকার ভাতা না দেওয়া.	জগদীশ বেসরা সহ ৩৪ জন।	বি.ডি.ও	বিশড়ি	মানবাজার-১নং।	

গ্রামীণ কর্মনিশ্চয়তা আইন ২০০৫, অভিযোগের তালিকা

জেলা — পুরুলিয়া

ক্রমিক নং	অভিযোগ	অভিযোগকারী	কাকে অভিযোগ জানানো হয়েছে	গ্রাম পঞ্চায়েত	ব্লক	ব্যবস্থা কি নেওয়া হয়েছে
৪১.	বেকার ভাতা না দেওয়া	নিতাই মাঝি সহ ৩২ জন	বি.ডি.ও	বিশরী	মানবাজার (১)	
৪২.	বেকার ভাতা না দেওয়া	নিতাই মাঝি সহ ৩৪ জন	বি.ডি.ও	বিশরী	মানবাজার (১)	
৪৩.	বেকার ভাতা না দেওয়া	নলিনলোচন মান্ডি সহ ৮৩ জন	বি.ডি.ও	বিশরী	মানবাজার (১)	
৪৪.	কাজের [illegible] জব কার্ড না দেওয়া	অতুল টুডু সহ ৮ জন	বি.ডি.ও	[illegible]	ঝালদা	
৪৫.	মজুরী / ক্ষতিপূরণ না দেওয়া	সরল মাহাত সহ ২৪ জন	বি.ডি.ও	পুঞ্চা	পুঞ্চা	
৪৬.	মজুরী / ক্ষতিপূরণ না দেওয়া	নারায়ণ মাহাত সহ ৭২ জন	বি.ডি.ও	পুঞ্চা	পুঞ্চা	
৪৭.	মজুরী / ক্ষতিপূরণ না দেওয়া	[illegible] মাহাত সহ ২ জন	বি.ডি.ও	পুঞ্চা	পুঞ্চা	
৪৮.	মজুরী / ক্ষতিপূরণ না দেওয়া	নারায়ণ মাহাত সহ ৮ জন	বি.ডি.ও	পুঞ্চা	পুঞ্চা	
৪৯.	মজুরী / ক্ষতিপূরণ না দেওয়া	নারায়ণ মাহাত সহ ৫ জন	বি.ডি.ও	পুঞ্চা	পুঞ্চা	
৫০.	মজুরী / ক্ষতিপূরণ না দেওয়া	নারায়ণ মাহাত সহ ৩ জন	বি.ডি.ও	পুঞ্চা	পুঞ্চা	

গ্রামীণ কর্মনিশ্চয়তা আইন ২০০৫, অভিযোগের তালিকা

জেলা — পুরুলিয়া

ক্রমিক নং	অভিযোগ	অভিযোগকারী	কাকে অভিযোগ জানানো হয়েছে	গ্রাম পঞ্চায়েত	ব্লক	ব্যবস্থা কি নেওয়া হয়েছে
৫১.	মজুরী / ক্ষতিপূরণ না দেওয়া	নারায়ণ মাহাত ও অন্য ৫৪ জন	পঞ্চায়েত সমিতি	পুঞ্চা	পুঞ্চা	
৫২.	মজুরী / ক্ষতিপূরণ না দেওয়া	নারায়ণ মাহাত ও অন্য ৫৩ জন	বি.ডি.ও	পুঞ্চা	পুঞ্চা	
৫৩.	মজুরী / ক্ষতিপূরণ না দেওয়া	জহুরলাল মাহাত ও অন্য	বি.ডি.ও	পায়রাচালী	পুঞ্চা	
৫৪.	মজুরী / ক্ষতিপূরণ না দেওয়া	লক্ষ্মীকান্ত মণ্ডল ও অন্য ৫২ জন	বি.ডি.ও	লাখড়া	পুঞ্চা	
৫৫.	মজুরী / ক্ষতিপূরণ না দেওয়া	মতিলাল হাঁসদা ও অন্য ২৫ জন	বি.ডি.ও	লাখড়া	পুঞ্চা	
৫৬.	মজুরী / ক্ষতিপূরণ না দেওয়া	তারাপতি মাহাতো	বি.ডি.ও	লাখড়া	পুঞ্চা	
৫৭.	মজুরী / ক্ষতিপূরণ না দেওয়া	নারায়ণ মাহাত ও অন্য ২ জন	বি.ডি.ও	পুঞ্চা	পুঞ্চা	
৫৮.	মজুরী / ক্ষতিপূরণ না দেওয়া	লক্ষণ মাহাত ও অন্য ৭ জন	পুলিশ	চেতনিয়া	মাঁতুড়ি	
৫৯.	মজুরী / ক্ষতিপূরণ না দেওয়া	কমল মান্ডি ও অন্য ৫ জন	বি.ডি.ও	মনিহারা	মাঁতুড়ি	
৬০.	মজুরী / ক্ষতিপূরণ না দেওয়া	লক্ষণ মাহাত ও অন্য ২ জন	বি.ডি.ও	চেতনিয়া	মাঁতুড়ি	

গ্রামীণ কর্মনিশ্চয়তা আইন ২০০৫, অভিযোগের তালিকা

জেলা — পুরুলিয়া

ক্রমিক নং	অভিযোগ	অভিযোগকারী	কাকে অভিযোগ জানানো হয়েছে	গ্রাম পঞ্চায়েত	ব্লক	ব্যবস্থা কি নেওয়া হয়েছে
৬১.	মজুরী / ক্ষতিপূরণ না দেওয়া	অনুমতি মাহাত সহ ৩৫ জন	বি. ডি. ও	বেড়াদা	বরাবাজার	
৬২.	মজুরী / ক্ষতিপূরণ না দেওয়া	সুশীল মাহাত সহ ৫ জন	বি. ডি. ও	নপাড়া	পুঞ্চা	
৬৩.	মজুরী / ক্ষতিপূরণ না দেওয়া	সুশীল মাহাত সহ ২২ জন	বি. ডি. ও	লপাড়া	পুঞ্চা	
৬৪.	মজুরী / ক্ষতিপূরণ না দেওয়া	শিবশঙ্কর মাঝি সহ ১১ জন	বি. ডি. ও	পুঞ্চা	পুঞ্চা	
৬৫.	মজুরী / ক্ষতিপূরণ না দেওয়া	সুধীর মুর্মু সহ ৪৪ জন	বি. ডি. ও	ধানাড়া	মানবাজার-১	
৬৬.	মজুরী / ক্ষতিপূরণ না দেওয়া	সুধীর মুর্মু সহ ২ জন	বি. ডি. ও	ধানাড়া	মানবাজার-১	
৬৭.	মজুরী / ক্ষতিপূরণ না দেওয়া	সুধীর ঘড়া সহ ১৭ জন	বি. ডি. ও	ধানাড়া	মানবাজার-১	
৬৮.	মজুরী / ক্ষতিপূরণ না দেওয়া	অনিল নাথ মুর্মু সহ ১৭ জন	বি. ডি. ও	ধানাড়া	মানবাজার-১	
৬৯.	মজুরী / ক্ষতিপূরণ না দেওয়া	অনিল নাথ মুর্মু সহ ৩২ জন	বি. ডি. ও	ধানাড়া	মানবাজার-১	
৭০.	কাজের বদলে ইস্যুকার্ড কাজ না দেওয়া হয়. মজুরী / ক্ষতিপূরণ না দেওয়া	নিরঞ্জন নস্কর সহ ২৮ জন	বি. ডি. ও	ধানাড়া	মানবাজার-১	

গ্রামীণ কর্মনিশ্চয়তা আইন ২০০৫, অভিযোগের তালিকা

জেলা: পুরুলিয়া

ক্রমিক নং	অভিযোগ	অভিযোগকারী	কাকে অভিযোগ জানানো হয়েছে	গ্রাম পঞ্চায়েত	ব্লক	ব্যবস্থা কি নেওয়া হয়েছে
৭১.	কাজের বরাদ্দ ইস্যু করে জব কার্ড না দেওয়া এবং মজুরী ক্ষতিপূরণ না দেওয়া	শ্রী সুধীর কুমার মুর্মু সহ ৪৭ জন	পি.ডি.ও	ধীমাড়া	মানবাজার ১নং	
৭২.	কাজ না দেওয়া এবং বেকার ভাতা না দেওয়া	নিতাই মাঝি সহ ৩৫ জন	পি.ডি.ও	পিসরী	মানবাজার ১নং	
৭৩.	কাজের জন্য আবেদন নিয়ে নোটিশ বোর্ডে না টাঙানো এবং কাজের স্থলে সুযোগ সুবিধা না রাখা	গৌতম দত্ত সহ ২ জন	পি.ডি.ও	পুঞ্চা	পুঞ্চা	
৭৪.	জব কার্ড তৈরির সময় মজুরী / ক্ষতিপূরণ না দেওয়া	প্রসন্ন মাহাতো সহ ২০৭ জন	পি.ডি.ও	জয়তি	পুঞ্চা	
৭৫.	কাজের আবেদন জমা না নেওয়া এবং জব কার্ড না দেওয়া	ফটিক বাদ্যে সহ ৫ জন	পি.ডি.ও	বড়িকাড়ী	সাঁতুড়ি	
৭৬.	মজুরী / ক্ষতিপূরণ না দেওয়া এবং কাজ না দেওয়া	মোতিলাল মাহাতো সহ ৩০ জন	পি.ডি.ও / প্রধান	ভেজুয়া	মানবাজার	
৭৭.	কাজের জন্য আবেদন নিয়ে নোটিশ বোর্ডে না টাঙানো এবং কাজের স্থলে সুযোগ সুবিধা না রাখা	সুহাসিনী হাঁসদা সহ ৩ জন	পি.ডি.ও	মড়তুলিয়া	সাঁতুড়ি	
৭৮.	যাতায়াত ভাতা না দেওয়া মজুরী / ক্ষতিপূরণ না দেওয়া	নারায়ণ মাহাতো সহ ৬৩ জন	পি.ডি.ও	পুঞ্চা	পুঞ্চা	

Annexure 4

Copies of Repeated Pleading for Restoration of Tribal Land Encroached by the Administration

To,
The O.C. Bandwan P.S.
Bandwan, Dt- purulia. West Bengal.

মহাশয়,

আমাদের বিনীত নিবেদন এই যে, আমরা ১) শ্রী বিপনাথ মান্ডি পিতা ৺সরূপ ২) শ্রী পতিনাথ মান্ডি পিতা- ৺সরূপ ৩) শ্রী পশুপতি মান্ডি পিতা- ৺সরূপ ৪) শ্রী ধনপতি মান্ডি পিতা ৺সরূপ ৫) শ্রী সিমন্ত মান্ডি পিতা- ৺সরূপ। বান্দোয়ান থানার অন্তর্গত কুঁচিয়া অঞ্চলের অধীন কুঁচিয়া মৌজার (স্থায়ী) আদিবাসী (সাঁওতাল) সম্প্রদায়ভুক্ত গরীব চাষী॥

কুঁচিয়া মৌজার মধ্যে হাল প্লট নং ১২৩৮/১২৫৬ পোড়া, ১৯৬৮ সালে এক একর জমি কোবালা দলিল মূল্যে আমার মাতার নামে ক্রয় করা হইয়াছে। বর্তমানে আমরা উক্ত জমির স্বত্বাধীকারি। কিন্তু আমাদের বিনা অনুমতিতে অনুমানিক ১৫-২০ ডে: জমি পুলিশ ক্যাম্পের অন্তর্ভুক্ত করা হয়েছে॥ তাই আমরা চাষ আবাদ করিতে পারছিনা॥

অতএব মহাশয়ের নিকট আমাদের প্রার্থনা এই যে, যাহাতে উক্ত রায়ত জমিটি নির্বিবাদে ছাড়িয়া দেওয়া হয় তার সু-ব্যবস্থা করিতে মর্জি হয়।

ইহার সহিত দলিলের এক কপি প্রমাণ সংযুক্ত করিলাম॥

মৌজা/জমির বিবরণ:-

১/ মৌজা- কুঁচিয়া, জে.এল.নং- ৯১

২/ হাল প্লট নং- ১২৩৮/১২৫৬

ইতি,
বিনীত,

প্রতিলিপি নিম্ন ঠিকানায় অবগতে প্রেরীত হইল:-

১. B.D.O. Bandwan Block
Bandwan Dt- purulia.
২. B.L. & L.R.O. Bandwan
Bandwan, Dt- purulia
৩. D.L & L.R.O. purulia
Dt- purulia.
৪. president/Secretary
A.B.A.V.P.
West Bengal Branch
P.O. - G.I.P. Colony
Jagacha. Howrah-4 (W.B.)

(১) শ্রী বিপনাথ মান্ডি
পি:- ৺স্বরূপ মান্ডি
(২) পতিনাথ মান্ডি
পিতা- ৺স্বরূপ মান্ডি
(৩) শ্রী পশুপতি মান্ডি
পি: ৺স্বরূপ মান্ডি
(৪) শ্রী ধনপতি মান্ডি
পি: ৺স্বরূপ মান্ডি
(৫) সিমন্ত মান্ডি
পিতা- ৺স্বরূপ মান্ডি

তারিখ
০১-০৯-২০০৭

To,

The S.P. purulia.

বিষয়:- পুলিশ ক্যাম্পের অন্তর্ভুক্ত রায়তী জমি নির্বিবাদে ছাড়িয়া দেওয়া হয় তার জন্য এই আবেদন পত্র।

মহাশয়,

আমাদের বিনীত নিবেদন এই যে, আমরা ১) শ্রী বিপিননাথ মান্ডি পিতা- ৺স্বরূপ ২) শ্রী শশিনাথ মান্ডি পিতা- ৺স্বরূপ ৩) শ্রী পশুপতি মান্ডি পিতা- ৺স্বরূপ ৪) শ্রী ধনপতি মান্ডি পিতা- ৺স্বরূপ ৫) শ্রী সিদাম মান্ডি পিতা- ৺স্বরূপ বান্দোয়ান থানার অন্তর্গত কুঁচিয়া অঞ্চলের অধীন কুঁচিয়া মৌজার স্থায়ী আদিবাসী সাঁওতাল সম্প্রদায়ভুক্ত গরীব চাষী।

আমাদের কুঁচিয়া মৌজার মধ্যে হাল প্লট নং ১২৩৬/১২৬৫ গোঃ ইং ১৯৬৮ সালে এক একর জমি কোবালা দলিল মূল্যে পিতার নামে ক্রয় করা হইয়াছে। বর্তমানে আমরা উক্ত জমির স্বত্বাধিকারী। কিন্তু আমাদের বিনা অনুমতিতে প্রায় ১৫-২০ ডেঃ জমি পুলিশ ক্যাম্পের অন্তর্ভুক্ত করা হয়েছে।

অতএব মহাশয়ের নিকট আমাদের প্রার্থনা এই যে, যাহাতে উক্ত রায়তী জমিটি নির্বিবাদে ছাড়িয়া দেওয়া হয় তাহার সুব্যবস্থা করিতে মর্জি হয়।

ইহার সহিত পর্চার জেরক্স সংযুক্ত করিলাম।

জমির বিবরণ

১. মৌজা:- কুঁচিয়া, জে.এল. নং- ৯৬

২. হাল প্লট নং:- ১২৩৬/১২৬৫

প্রকাশ থাকে যে, গত ইংরেজী ০৫-১০-২০০৭ তারিখে এই বিষয়ে B.L&L.R.O. বান্দোয়ান মহাশয়ের নিকট আবেদন করা হইয়াছিল কিন্তু B.L&L.R.O মহাশয় আমাদের আবেদনের কোন দৃষ্টি না দেওয়ার জন্য আপনার নিকট আবেদন করিতে বাধ্য হইলাম। আমাদের বিশ্বাস এই আবেদনে আপনি অবশ্যই দৃষ্টি আকর্ষণ করিবেন।

নিবেদন,
ইতি,

১. শ্রী বিপিন [illegible] মান্ডি
২. [illegible] মান্ডি
৩. শ্রী পশুপতি মান্ডি
৪. [illegible] মান্ডি
৫. শ্রী [illegible] মান্ডি

পিতা- ৺স্বরূপ মান্ডি
গ্রাম+পোঃ- কুঁচিয়া
ব্লক+থানা- বান্দোয়ান
জেলা- পুরুলিয়া

প্রতিলিপি নিম্ন ঠিকানায় অবগতার্থে প্রেরিত হইল:-

১. প্রতি,
সভাপতি/সম্পাদক মহাশয়
পশ্চিম বঙ্গ খেড়িয়া-শবর কল্যাণ সমিতি
গ্রাম+পোঃ+ রাজনওয়াগড়, জেলা- পুরুলিয়া।

আবেদন পত্রটি ইংরেজী [illegible]/১০/০৮ তারিখে পাঠানো হয়েছে।

প্রতি,

মাননীয় সম্পাদক মহাশয় সংবাদ প্রতিদিন

প্রসঙ্গ — পুলিশ ক্যাম্পের জন্য জমি দখল, তীব্র ক্ষোভ

গত ইংরেজি ১২-০৯-২০০৮ শুক্রবার প্রতিদিন সংবাদ পত্রের ৩য় পৃষ্ঠায় প্রকাশিত প্রতিবেদনের প্রেক্ষিতে এই চিঠি। প্রথমেই বলি, সংবাদটি প্রকাশের জন্য সাংবাদিক অচিন দত্ত মহাশয়কে ধন্যবাদ জানাচ্ছি॥ ওই সংবাদের প্রথম অনুচ্ছেদের শেষ প্রসঙ্গে জানাই, জমি খোয়ানো মানুষজন আলোচনায় বসতে রাজি নয় — এ তথ্য সঠিক নয়।

বান্দোয়ানের ও.সি এবং ভূমি ও ভূমি আধিকারিক মহাশয়ের নিকট আমাদের আবেদন পত্র দেওয়া সত্ত্বেও কর্ণপাত করেননি। এমনকি এবিষয়ে আমরা আধিকারিকের নিকট খোঁজ নিলে আমাদেরকে একটিও [illegible] দেখানো হয়। প্রশাসনের পুলিশ [illegible] ভয় দেখিয়ে জোর পূর্বক আমাদের জমি দখল করেছেন।

বান্দোয়ানের ভূমি ও ভূমি আধিকারিক মাননীয় শ্রী কৃষ্ণ সাধন দাস মহাশয় তাঁর পিঠ বাঁচানোর জন্য সাংবাদিক মহাশয়কে ভুল তথ্য পেশ করেছেন॥ দয়া করে এটুকু সংশোধন করুন। আপনারা তো চান, "জমি খোয়ানো মানুষজন বিচার পাক"॥

ইতি,

বিপুনাথ মান্ডি, সতিনাথ মান্ডি
পশুপতি মান্ডি, দিনপতি মান্ডি
সিমন্ত মান্ডি॥
গ্রাম+ব্লক - কুঁচিয়া
থানা - বান্দোয়ান, জেলা - পুরুলিয়া

তারিখ
২০/০৯/২০০৮

পুলিশ ক্যাম্পের জন্য জমি দখল, তীব্র ক্ষোভ

অচিন দত্ত • বান্দোয়ান

১১ সেপ্টেম্বর : সিঙ্গুর নন্দীগ্রাম নয়, শিবায়নও নয়। পুলিশের তাঁবু করার জন্য জোর করে জমি দখল করার অভিযোগ উঠল। ঘটনাটি পুরুলিয়ার মাওবাদী উপদ্রুত বান্দোয়ানের কুচিয়া এলাকায়। ঘটনায় রীতিমতো ক্ষুব্ধ জমিহারারা। অভিযোগের সত্যতা স্বীকার করেছে প্রশাসনও। সব মিলিয়ে কুচিয়ার আদিবাসীরা ক্ষোভে ফুঁসছেন পুলিশের বিরুদ্ধে। বান্দোয়ানের বিডিও প্রসেনজিৎ দাস বলেছেন, "জমি হারাদের বিষয়টি ওই সময় পঞ্চায়েত সমিতির সিপিএম সহ-সভাপতি রতন সরেন এবং ভূমি আধিকারিককে সরেজমিনে খতিয়ে দেখে নিষ্পত্তির জন্য জানানো হয়েছিল।" বান্দোয়ান ভূমি ও ভূমি উন্নয়ন দফতরের আধিকারিক কৃষ্ণসাধন দাস বলেন, "কুচিয়া সিআরপি ক্যাম্প তৈরির সময় জমি চিহ্নিতকরণ করে দেওয়া হয়েছিল। পরে বাউন্ডারি ওয়াল দেওয়ার সময় কয়েকজন ব্যক্তির জায়গা ঢুকে যায়। জমি খোয়ানো মানুষজন আলোচনায় বসতে রাজি নয়।"

মাওবাদী [illegible] বান্দোয়ানের ভোমরাগোড়ায় মাওবাদী হামলায় সস্ত্রীক সিপিএম নেতা খুন, গুড়পাড়া সিআরপিএফ ক্যাম্পে বিস্ফোরণ, দুয়ারসিনিতে বনবিভাগের ছটি আবাসন উড়িয়ে দেওয়ার মতো পরপর কয়েকটি নাশকতা সংঘটিত হওয়ায় সিপিএম নেতা ও সরকারি উদ্যোগে ২০০৭ সালে সিআরপি সাতটি ক্যাম্প নির্মাণ হয় কুচিয়ায়। মেদিনীপুরের লালগড়-বেলপাহাড়ি-কাঁকড়াঝোড় জঙ্গল থেকে ঝাড়গ্রাম হয়ে পুরুলিয়ার বান্দোয়ান জঙ্গল মহলের গুড়পানা থেকে সোজা পথে কুচিয়া হয়ে ভোমরাগোড়া থেকে পাহাড়ি জঙ্গল পথে ঝাড়খণ্ডের পটমদা এলাকা মাওবাদী করিডোর হিসাবে চিহ্নিত। তাই মাওবাদী হামলা ও গতিবিধি রুখতে গঠিত হয় কুচিয়া ক্যাম্প।

কুচিয়ার বাসিন্দা বিফনান মাঝি, পতিনাথ মাঝি এবং পশুপতি মাঝি-সহ পাঁচজন সংশ্লিষ্ট বিভাগীয় কর্তাদের লিখিত অভিযোগে জানিয়েছেন, কুচিয়া মৌজার মধ্যে কিছু জমির মালিকানা থাকা সত্ত্বেও জোরপূর্বক কিছুটা জায়গা পুলিশ ক্যাম্পের অন্তর্ভুক্ত করা হয়েছে। ২০০৭ সাল থেকে আপত্তি জানিয়ে আসছেন তাঁরা।

Index